SOVIET POLICY TOWARDS THE ARAB-ISRAELI CONFLICT 1948-1988

Soviet Policy Towards The Arab—Israeli Conflict 1948-1988

M. Mahmood

GIAN PUBLISHING HOUSE
NEW DELHI-110002

GIAN PUBLISHING HOUSE
4348, Madan Mohan Street
4-C Ansari Road, Darya Ganj,
New Delhi-110002

ISBN 81—212—0247—7

PRINTED IN INDIA

Published by Mrs. Gayatri Garg for Gian Publishing House, New Delhi
and Printed at Godwall Printers, Delhi.

Preface

The present study represents a modest attempt at a theoretical understanding of 'Soviet Policy towards the Arab-Israeli Conflict' and comprehending the dynamics of Soviet intervention in the area in a historical perspective of superpower confrontation since World War II.

The vicissitudes of Soviet diplomacy during the Cold War, detente and post-detente periods have been focussed upon. Accordingly, Soviet forward policy during 1955-56 ; cautious and hesitant engagement during 1967-73 ; measured neglect during 1979-84, and finally, the ad-hocist, contingent, piecemeal and ultra-conservative nature of Soviet formulations towards a regional settlement have been discussed at length. The study comes to an end with a survey of the emerging trends in Soviet West-Asia policy since the advent of the Gorbachev era.

For all the encouragement and moral support I have received in the preparation of this study, I am greatly indebted to Professor Irfan Habib, Coordinator, Centre of Advanced Study, Department of History, Aligarh Muslim University ; Professor M.M. Puri, Punjab University, Chandigarh ; and Professor Haridwar Rai Visiting Professor, Department of Political Science, North-eastern Hill University, Shillong. I am also indebted to Professor M.S. Agwani. Vice Chancellor, Jawaharlal Nehru University, New Delhi and Professor S.A.H. Haqqi for giving me the benefit of their critical comments.

M. MAHMOOD

Contents

		Page
	Preface	v
	CHAPTER	
I.	**On Studying Soviet Foreign Policy**	1—11
	Contending Approaches (2) ; Scope, Source and Method (8).	
II.	**The USSR and the Arab World 1948-1955**	12—35
	West-Asia in World Politics 12 ; Soviet Policy in West Asia 1945—1955 (16) ; Soviet Approach towards the Arab World (16).	
III.	**Forward Policy 1956-1966**	36—68
	The Suez Crisis 1956 (36); Soviet Reaction (41); The Diplomatic Phase (44) ; Deliberation at the UN (52) ; The Suez War (56) ; The Arab-Israeli Conflict 1957-67 (63).	
IV.	**The War of 1973 and Reappraisal**	69—82
	The Syrian Crisis 1967 (60) ; The War of June 1967 (75) ; The Security Council Resolution 242 (79).	

V. **Diplomatic Stalemate 1968-1972** 83—103

Soviet Diplomatic Offensive (83) ; Four-Power Talks and Rogers' Initiative (89); Soviet Intervention in the Suez Crisis of 1970 (92) ; Rogers' Peace and the Ceasefire (97) ; Search for an Interim Settlement (100).

VI. **The War of 1973 and After** 104—125

Background (104) ; Soviet Role (113) ; The UN Resolution 338 (117); Threat of Soviet Intervention (119); Assessment of the Soviet Role (121).

VII. **For Status Quo : Soviet Peace Moves Since 1948** 126—148

Early Soviet Attitudes (126); Israeli Nationhood, Direct Talks (127) ; The Question of Boundaries, Refugees (128); Jerusalem (130) ; Jordan Waters, International Waterways (131) ; Soviet Line on a Political Settlement since 1967 (132) : Soviet Preferences since 1973 (137) ; Attitude towards the Palestinian Movement (140) ; The Advent of Gorbachev Era (143).

VIII. **Conclusion** 149—157

Select Bibliography 159—168

Index 169—171

CHAPTER I

On Studying Soviet Foreign Policy

The study of foreign policy is a subfield of the broader field of international relations. The analysis of foreign policies, at the international level and from the vantage point of powers, makes it possible to understand the anarchy of order that is the international system and the maze that is international politics. Status inequalities and uneven distribution of resources among the sovereign entities are hallmarks of this system. The major and super-powers, who occupy a central place in this system, are primarily guided in their external conduct by the goals of self-preservation and self-extension. But they have also developed, at the same time, a vital stake in the preservation and maintenance of the international system. In this context, foreign policies of interventionist great powers assume great significance in relation to the genesis, development, management, containment and/or resolution of regional conflicts which often pose a serious threat to regional stability and/or international peace and security. Hence the rationale of the present study.

Contending Approaches

It has been said that where the Soviet Union is concerned, "there are no degrees of knowledge, only degrees of ignorance".[1] Daniel Bell about a quarter century ago observed that "The road to hell must be paved twice over with thousands of books claiming to discover the truth about Russia."[2] Today, however, such excessive pessimism would seem to be misplaced. Although our knowledge of Soviet foreign policy since World War-II is still far from wide, there are by now enough pieces of evidence which, seen through an appropriate theoretical framework, yield valuable insights into its complexities.[3]

A student of Soviet foreign policy is confronted at the very outset with the basic question of approach and method, as no analytical enterprise can do without a theoretical framework, whether explicit or implicit. In the recent past, a great debate has taken place between the classical and scientific schools in international relations, closely following an earlier debate between the idealist and realist schools within the classical tradition. The field is, thus, marked by a plethora of approaches, methods and conceptual framework. However, the emphasis has recently shifted from single-track approaches and unicausal theories to an acceptance of ecclecticism and diversity. This shift seems to be in consonance with the diversity and complexity of the present-day international relations. Gone are days of single-factorial explanatory hypotheses. Competing conceptual frameworks and methodologies today supplement and complement each other. No single factor is now regarded as sufficient to explain all the complex phenomena of international interaction.

Out of this diversity, we may single out two major approaches which were till recently in vogue in the Western world : the realist or power-political approach and the ideological approach.

According to the realist school, the USSR has nothing unique about its foreign policy and its diplomacy does not differ fundamentally from that of the other nation-states.

Soviet foreign policy is the lineal descendent of Tsarist foreign policy, motivated more by geopolitical considerations than by any transcendental ideology or moral purpose. The Soviet Union, like Tsarist Russia, continues to preserve, enhance and expand its power and influence beyond its geographical boundaries. As Lord Curzon once wrote : "So far from regarding the foreign policy of Russia as consistent, or remorseless, or profound, I believe it to be a hand-to-mouth policy, a policy of waiting upon events, profiting by the blunders of others and as often of committing the like herself."[4] This school emphasizes the primacy of the national interest of the USSR as a great power and minimizes the role of ideology in the formulation of policy or regards it merely as an adjunct of Soviet power.

The ideological school places primary emphasis on Soviet ideology as the sole determinant of Soviet foreign policy. It sees in the USSR a unique ideological state, motivated not by egocentric values of the traditional nation-state but by certain transcendental humanitarian and internationalist values. The value system of Marxism-Leninism is said to give its policy a dynamic character which radically differentiates it from Russian imperial policy. While its strategy follows a single purpose, its tactics may be flexible admitting of temporary bargains and compromises. This school cites V.I. Lenin's early definition of Soviet foreign policy in 1920 in which he ridiculed the refusal "to temporise and compromise with possible allies" and defended the idea that at times "we might have to go in zig-zags, sometimes retreating our steps, sometimes abandoning the course already selected and trying out various others".[5] The exponents of this approach see conscious purposiveness and a consistent pursuit of the goal of world revolution which includes the many compromises and zig-zags recommended by Lenin in 1920. Thus, "peaceful co-existence" may be seen as a temporary phase on the road to the final victory of communism. On the other hand, the radical right view of Soviet policy sees Soviet ideology merely as a "method of conflict in space over a sustained period of time", that is, "a method of protracted conflict".[6] This view might have been somewhat true during Stalin's life-time and the early phase of the Cold War. It is no longer true today as it presupposes permanent exclusion of negotiation, compromise, peaceful co-existence and co-operation between rival social systems. The advent of the thermonuclear age has wrought a fundamental transformation in Soviet perspectives on international relations. As the nuclear weapons have made a war between the great powers impossible, the Cold War has been replaced by detente in their relations recommending negotiation, rather than confrontation as a means of resolving their conflicts.

Today, the interest-ideology dichotomy seems to be unreal and their antithesis sterile. Both the schools have, therefore, tended to recognize the inadequacy of their determinism and the need for a more expansive approach to understand the new realities. This leads us to a third approach which integrates interest and ideology[7]. Both the basic Soviet national interests and the basic tenets of Soviet faith are regarded as representing important sources of Soviet behaviour in world affairs. This also conforms with the official Soviet view that there can be no clash between Marxism-Leninism and the national interests of the Soviet State as the latter are supposed to subserve the former. Nevertheless, a possible conflict between the two has been recognized from the days of the Bolshevik Revolution and on many occasions ideology has been adjusted to reality. Adam B. Ulam is a prominent exponent of this line who in his numerous writings has described the amalgam of belief, experience, acuteness and misperception which underlay Soviet calculations. According to Kurt London, "It is like two sides of a coin—the face of revolutionary interests and that of state interests merge to make one unity, Soviet foreign policy. We cannot separate the sides, but from time to time we seem to see one more clearly or frequently than the other."[8] Thus, Soviet foreign policy cannot be explained either in terms of geopolitics alone or ideological commitments alone. Either tends to overlook the objective changes in the domestic and international environment which necessitate modification in belief, behaviour and policies.

The concept of national interest, despite its analytical fuzziness and inadequacy to describe all phenomena of foreign policy, has been a viable concept to define and justify national objectives. Hans J. Morgenthau, the exponent of the "realist" theory of international politics, defines "interest" in terms of power. He holds out the concept as "the main sign-post that helps political realism to find its way through the landscape of international politics."[9] He defined "power" as the ability to influence the minds and actions of others, exercised by any means whether psychological, political or military. Morgenthau's theory has been attacked not so much for its explanatory limitations as for its normative orientations. It has made a number of useful contributions to the discipline : (a) it explicitly shows the value of generalization ; (b) it emphasizes the fact that inter-state relations, in their essence, display patterns of behaviour and recurrence ; (c) it defines the core of the subject as the sources of state behaviour (i.e., the search for power and influence) and resulting patterns of relations (i.e., spheres of influence/balance of power); and (d) it explores the causes of war and conditions of peace in the international system.[10]

The deficiency of Morgenthau's formulation has been sought to be removed by such more elaborate conceptual scheme as one formulated by Arnold Wolfers[11] who classifies the goals of foreign policy as self-preservation, self-extension and self-abnegation, or another by Robert E. Osgood[12] who combined the moral and material in his taxonomy of foreign policy goals and thus made it more acceptable. According to Sprouts, the "Wolfers' scheme has the merit of breaking out of the sterile axiom that all politics is a struggle for power, and its equally sterile corollary that maximization of power is the highest goal of foreign policy. The Wolfers' scheme could be used to compare a single state's foreign policy at different periods in its history, or to compare the policies of two or more states in the same or different historical periods."[13]

If a taxonomy of foreign-policy goals based on the notion of national interest may serve as a key to foreign policy motivations in general then the concept of "imperialism" may illuminate the motivations of the policy of a "patron" state in relation to a "client" state. As defined by Benjamin J. Cohen, imperialism is ". . . those particular relationships between inherently unequal nations which involve effective subjugation, the actual exercise of influence over behaviour."[14]

What role does ideology play in the information and execution of foreign policy today? We may profit greatly from the findings of two leading Western scholars of current Soviet foreign policy. Zimmerman in his path-breaking work[15] has surveyed the evolution of Soviet elite and specialist perspectives on the international system and international relations during the Khrushchevian and post-Khrushchevian periods. He has highlighted three points: (1) An evidence of a movement towards a more empirical appraisal of the international system. Soviet perceptions showed *growing convergence with the Western concept and perceptions.* The new appreciation of the complexities of international reality has entailed a progressive discarding of heretofore sacrosanct doctrines with their simplistic zero-sum games by the ruling elite and academic specialists alike. (2) Although it was difficult to overcome or abandon altogether the ideology-induced habit of viewing international relations in terms of class struggle and world historical-revolutionary process, *the nation-states were recognized as the principal actors in the international system.* With the advent of the atomic age [after the Cuban Missile Crisis Khrushchev had declared that "the atomic bomb does not recognize the class principle" and that the workers were likely to lose more than their chains in a future nuclear war][16] and with the prolongation of the Soviet time-span for the ultimate arrival of communism at home [by inventing the concept of a "developed" socialist state] and internationally [through the growing separation of world politics from world historical process] there has been a *demonstrable erosion of the influence of ideology on foreign policy.* Much of the importance given to the role of ideology in current Soviet Foreign policy is, therefore, misplaced. Ideology has ceased to be the sole, even major determinant of policy. Many of the sacred doctrines of the past and even some basic Leninist postulates and perspectives have become redundant in the "post-imperialist" era. This does not, however, mean total erosion or an end of the ideology. Ideology now serves less as a *guide of action* but more as a rationalizer and legitimator. Ideology also continues to serve as a methodology, as the language of analysis. However doctrinal purity is sacrificed as soon as the rational and efficient pursuit of foreign policy goals requires it. As a global power with global responsibilities the Soviet Union has increasingly realized that it has a stake in the maintenance rather than destruction of the international system.

Similarly, Aspaturian traces the erosion of ideology in the growing fragmentation of the post-Stalin decision making process, the loosening of the Soviet bloc, the Sino-Soviet dispute, and the globalization of Soviet foreign policy. Instead of "erosion" he recommends the use of the term "de-ideologization" to define the process whereby "foreign policy goals have been progressively disengaged from ideological norms." Far from discarding ideology as a variable, he holds that Soviet foreign policy has always been the product of ideology in combination with other variables : capabilities, perceived opportunities, personalities, extra-volitional institutional and functional restraints and the existing correlation of forces in the international field.[17]

Zimmerman is of the view that "one ought to accord as much weight to international system-level explanations of Soviet foreign policy as one would in the case of any other state".[18] He has called attention to a number of empirical generalizations which he claims to have derived from systematic observation of Soviet international behaviour and which explain the conservative nature of current Soviet foreign policy, namely : that the international performance capabilities of the Soviet Union are not distinctive; that the Soviet leaders have a stake in their reputation for credibility ; that the Soviet attitude in international life is extremely cautious and avoids risky ventures; and that Soviet foreign policy is, to some extent, reactive to external developments and concerned with the preservation of the elite and enhancement of its prestige at home and abroad. This is the most pronounced trend of the post-Brezhnev era.

In sum, Soviet motivation seems to be a product of the operational mix of a number of variables—the domestic institutional structure and accompanying roles and interests, personalities and idiosyncracies of the decision-makers, the objective historical events taking place in the international environment, and the elite's belief system. These variables as building blocks remain constant but their content and proportional combination at any given time are changing. It is their content and combination in a given situation that produces the motivation of the Soviet Union as an actor in the international system. However, no general theory of Soviet foreign policy have been possible yet. The field abounds in competing theoretical expositions as well as empirical case studies. Our generalizations about Soviet external behaviour may therefore be regarded as tentative and imperfect at best.

Scope, Sources and Method

This study shall address itself to exploring the themes of relevance of Marxism-Leninism to the Soviet conduct in West Asia, the theme of continuity and change in the Soviet line and the theme of spontaniety and consciousness in Soviet action.

Soviet policy towards the Arab-Israeli conflict is subordinated to Soviet global and regional policies. The specific Soviet attitude to the Arab-Israeli conflict at a given time is determined by global and regional considerations of Soviet policy. Soviet global and regional policies are determined by Soviet global and regional interests as perceived and formulated by the Soviet leadership. An identification of interests may lead to formulation of national goals, objectives and preferences, long-term and short-term, to secure and promote such interests. The pursuit of these objectives is always circumscribed by the domestic factors, availability of resources, the regional environment and actors, and the global environment and actors.

Soviet involvement in the Arab-Israeli conflict has been studied during the two distinct phases of post-World War II history. In the East-West Cold-War phase the conflict played an instrumental role in the promotion of Soviet strategic and political interests. But it tended to prove detrimental to these interests during the phase of the superpower detente.

The transitional period from 1955 to 1967 in West Asia is remarkable for resurgence of Arab nationalism, growth of non-alignment and rising influence of the Soviet Union in the area in return of arms deals, aid and trade and diplomatic support to the Arabs against the West and Israel. Its policy of regional polarization ended with the Arab defeat in the

June 1967 War and temporary loss of prestige. The turbulent period from 1967 to 1973 saw the Soviet Union confront a serious dilemma of reconciling her global commitments under its incipient detente with the United States with her risky regional commitments. During this period the Soviet Union was forced to formulate and implement a policy of temporization vis-a-vis the Arab-Israeli conflict, namely, by negating the Arab option for a military solution, by limiting the arms supply, and by stressing the needs for a political settlement of the conflict. In retrospect, Soviet inventions in the crises of 1956, 1967, 1970, and 1973 appear to be motivated by the desire of either enhancing or preventing the total loss of Soviet influence, rather than by a desire to tilt the balance of power in favour of the Arabs. However, the exclusion of the Soviet Union from the Arab-Israeli sector in the wake of 1973 War has not distracted it from continuing its search for influence in the region. But inward-looking pragmatism seems to be the dominant trend of post-detente Soviet policy.

This study combines the historical-descriptive with the analytical method, though, in fairness, full justice cannot be done to either. So far as the sources are concerned, it heavily relies on the official statements of the Soviet Party and Government. Official statements, documents and speeches have been taken from the *Current Digest of the Soviet Press*, *Daily Review*, and BBC *Summary of the World Broadcasts* Part I and Part IV.[19] Next in importance are the writings of Soviet commentators and specialists, which explain, elaborate and rationalize the official policies. This material has been taken from the *New Times* (weekly), *International Affairs* (Monthly) and the *World Marxist Review* (Monthly) and occasional monographs.[20] Press and radio commentaries often serve as source material but require careful interpretation to separate facts from propaganda. When analysed in the context of unfolding events and Soviet response to them, Soviet open communications do seem to reveal the basic approach of the regime to foreign affairs, its patterns of reasoning and the fundamental assumptions on which it acts. Whenever a contradiction appears between the spoken word and the actual deed, Soviet deeds would appear to be a better guide to motivation. Lastly, the records of the

UN Security Council and the General Assembly have been utilized.

Chapter II provides a general background to the evolution of Soviet policy towards the region and the Palestine question. Chapters III to VII represent substantive case studies of the Soviet role during the 1956, 1967, 1970 and 1973 crises, and of the Soviet line on a political settlement in the area during 1948-1984 some broad conclusions are summed up in the last chapter. Together, these chapters provide a thorough, well-documented analysis of the conduct of Soviet Arab-policy during the period 1948-84.

REFERENCES

1. Robin Edmonds, *Soviet Foreign Policy, 1962-1973. The Paradox of Superpower* (London, 1975), p. 8.
2. Daniel Bell, "Ten Theories in Search of Reality : The Prediction of Soviet Behaviour in Social Sciences" in Bell, *The End of Ideology* (Glencoe, 1960), pp. 300-334.
3. See William Zimmerman, "What Scholars know about Soviet Foreign Policy". *International Journal* 37 (Spring 1982).
4. George N. Curzon, *Russia in Central Asia* (London, 1889), p. 315 ; other specimens in this category : Philip E. Mosley, *The Kremlin and World Politics*, Studies in Soviet Policy and Action (New York, 1960) ; M.D. Shulman, *Soviet Foreign Policy Reappraised* (London, 1963) ; D.F. Fleming, *Cold War and Its Origins*, 1917-1960 (London, 1963).
5. V.I. Lenin, *Left-Wing Communism - An Infantile Disorder* (1920) in *Collected Works* 31, p. 70.
6. Robert Strausz-Hupe, William R. Kintner, James E. Dougherty and Alvin J. Cottrel, *Protracted Conflict* (New York, 1959).
7. Cf. Adam, B. Ulam, *Expansion and Co-existence*. Soviet Foreign Policy 1917-73 (New York, 1974) ; Adam Bromke, "Ideology and National Interest in Soviet Foreign Policy". *International Journal* 22 (Autumn 1967) ; Zafar Imam, *Ideology and Reality in Soviet Policy in Asia* : Indo-Soviet Relations 1947-60 (Delhi, 1975) ; Kurt London, ed., *The Soviet Union* : A Half Century of Communism (Baltimore, 1968).
8. London, ed., (*note* 7), p. 328.
9. Hans J. Morgenthau, *Politics Among Nations* 5th ed. (New York, 1973), p. 5.

10. Cf. James N. Rosenau, "National Interest" in *International Encyclopedia of the Social Sciences* XI, pp. 35-40.
11. Arnold Wolfers, "The Goals of Foreign Policy", in Wolfers, ed., *Discord and Collaboration* (Baltimore, 1962), pp. 67-80.
12. Robert E. Osgood, *Ideas and Self-Interest in American Foreign Relations* (Chicago, 1953).
13. Harold Sprout and Margaret Sprout, *Foundations of International Politics* (Princeton, 1962), p. 122.
14. Benjamin J. Cohen, *The Question of Imperialism* : The Political Economy of Dominance and Dependence (New York, 1973), p. 15. The pioneering work in the study of inter-Nation influence is David J. Singer, "Inter-Nation Influence : A Formal Model", in Rosenau, ed. *International Politics and Foreign Policy*. See also Richard W. Cottam, *Competitive Interference and Twentieth Century Diplomacy* (Pittsburg, 1967) ; Alvin Z. Rubenstein, ed., *Soviet and Chinese Influence in the Third World* (New York, 1975) ; and Rubenstein, *Red Star on the Nile* : Soviet-Egyptian relationship since the June War (Princeton, 1977).
15. William Zimmerman, *Soviet Perspectives on International Relations 1956-1967* (Princeton, 1969).
16. Cited in *World Marxist Review* 5 (December 1962), p. 6.
17. Vernon V. Aspaturian, "Soviet Foreign Policy at the Crossroads : Conflict and/or Collaboration". *International Organization* 23 (Summer 1969), pp. 592-596. The end-of-ideology thesis propounded by Daniel Bell and others in the west is simply inapplicable to Soviet domestic and foreign policies. As formulated in the West, the thesis (1) marks only *decline* of political ideology and corresponding rise of political pragmatism and (2) it does not mean an end of the ideology altogether but convergence of existing ideologies. On the other hand, the logic of a single, sacrosanct official ideology is inherent in the Soviet political system. In the absence of democratic means of legitimation, the official ideology alone legitimates and sustains the Soviet establishment and its policies. Any radical transformation of this formal ideology or its dilution must entail the radical transformation of the system itself.
18. William Zimmerman, "Elite Perspectives and the Explanations of Soviet Foreign Policy". *Journal of International Affairs* 26 (1970), pp. 84-98.
19. On the problem of interpreting Soviet documents see Zimmerman (note 15), pp. 9-10.
20. About the value of writings of Soviet specialists see *Mizan Newsletter* No. 12 (December 1959), pp. 4-7; Thomas P. Thornton, *The Third World in Soviet perspective* (Princeton, 1964), pp. x-xiii.

CHAPTER II

The USSR and the Arab World 1948-1955

West Asia in World Politics

No survey of the evolution of Soviet policy in West Asia can be meaningful without an account of factors and forces which make the region one of the focal areas in world politics, namely, its geostrategic location, its oil and natural resources, its internal divisions and conflicts, and its ideological movements that have revolutionized its politics and society.

Geographically, the region is situated at the intersection of three continents and three oceans giving it a position of centrality and making it a bridge connecting Europe, Asia and Africa. Before the advent of the jet age, it was really the crossroads of the world. It is still a highly important communications hub and a key area in transportation as land, sea and air routes from Europe to Asia pass through it. It is this centrality of location which accounts for its geopolitical significance. Its two strategic waterways—the Turkish Straits and the Suez Canal—have traditionally been an object of great power rivalry, as in conventional strategy they were regarded as keys to the control of the entire Mediterranean and the West Asian region.

The oil and natural resources of the region are yet another strategic factor. Some basic facts about West Asian/North African oil are that (1) since the discovery of oil in this area in the early days of the present century its production has kept increasing steadily till at present the region has become the largest oil producing area outside the communist world and contains estimated reserves of about 399,000 million barrels of crude which is about 76 per cent of the non-Communist World's proven oil reserves. The area also has an estimated 30 per cent of the World's gas reserves. (2) About 75 per cent of Europe's fuel requirements and about 80 per cent of Japan's needs are supplied by West Asian oil. (3) In terms of production cost, the West Asian oil is the cheapest in the world market. (4) Oil is steadily displacing coal as a source of energy while providing a base for numerous petrochemical industries. Advances in hydroelectric and nuclear energy technologies have not lessened the dependence of the industrialized countries on oil. (5) Supplies of oil from West Asia/North Africa are conditioned not only by normal commercial considerations but also by internal political conditions and international relations in this volatile area. (6) Among all the oil-extracting countries in the region the USA has the dominant interest in its oil-fields and their proceeds. (7) Within ten years after the end of World War II the revenues from oil concessions overshadowed all other revenues of the oil-producing countries in the area. By 1967, these revenues reached an imposing total figure of 2.9 billion dollars. Oil revenues due to the spiralling prices in the wake of energy crisis of the 1970s have made the oil-producing countries powerful independent actors in inter-national and regional politics. The heavy dependence of the USA, European Community and Japan on the West Asian/North African oil for their industries and strategic requirements has contributed to making oil one of the main determining factors of Western and American policy towards the region. America strives to maintain its influence with the producer countries in order to safeguard the oilfields and installations in the area, to ensure availability of transit facilities and to prevent major crises, breakdowns or interruptions which could disrupt oil supplies which keep the Western industrial machine going. The Soviet Union on the other hand, was mainly interested in the region because of security considerations and did not have a stake in its oil, as it was self-sufficient in oil.[1]

However, of late, the strategic significance of the area in a military sense has definitely declined. It ceased to be a crossroads long ago and its military bases and naval facilities are no longer indispensable to the great powers in an era of strategic mobility. Its present political importance owes to its oil resources and to the superpower competition for influence in the area and in the world at large.

The ideational elements[2] accounting for dynamism in the region's politics are nationalism, non-alignment, anti-imperialism, anti-colonialism, anti-racialism and quest for rapid modernization and development. The ideological ferment in the Arab world since World War II was the result of its long encounter with Western imperialism. Foreign domination in West Asia was caused by the three factors of geography, ethnicity and economics. European penetration of these lands had begun as early as the eighteenth century with trade and commerce. As the Ottoman Empire decayed, the Europeans extracted economic concessions, imposed capitulations and established extra-territorial rights and privileges for themselves. Then the growing needs of the industrializing Western Europe for sources of cheap raw materials and outlets for their manufactures brought colonialism to the area. In due course European powers established their respective protectorates and spheres of influence. The victorious powers in World War I assumed direct or indirect rule over the countries of the Fertile Crescent as a White Man's burden. Thus, with a few exceptions, the entire region was subjected to ruthless economic exploitation and political and cultural subjugation.

The twentieth century witnessed the growth of national self-consciousness among the colonial and subject peoples who began to assert their right to self-determination and independence.

Nationalism and national liberation movements gained momentum in West Asia during the inter-war period. With the Egyptian revolution of 1952, the Arab nationalist movement took to radicalism and revolutionism. In the East-West Cold War the nationalist regimes chose to be non-aligned to safeguard their independence, sovereignty and freedom of action.

West Asia may be described as the Balkans of the late twentieth century due to its geographical diffusion and internal conflicts, the most destabilizing of them being the Arab-Israeli conflict. Israel was created by the Western powers as their outpost in West Asia to serve as a watchdog of the Western interests in the area. The Arabs have since then faced a permanent threat of Israeli expansion and the unresolved problem of more than two million Palestinians uprooted from their homeland.

To the Arab-Israeli factor of instability may be added inter-Arab conflicts. There exist centripetal and centrifugal forces and tensions between pan-Arabism and local nationalisms, between radicalism and conservatism, and between monarchism and republicanism. These divisions have drawn the external powers into regional politics and inclined them to take sides in conformity with their strategic and political objectives.

The Suez War resulted in the elimination of the European powers from the region and brought in two rival superpowers—the USA and the USSR. The USA, as hitherto the dominant regional power in succession to Great Britain, has enjoyed well-entrenched positions and has acquired relatively permanent politico-strategic-economic interests in the area which may be summed up broadly as : (1) preservation, consolidation and strengthening of Israel as a bastion of Western influence ; (2) maintenance of control over the oil resources of the area and protection of the friendly Arab regimes ; (3) containment and/or elimination of the Soviet Union from the region by all means short of direct confrontation ; and (4) establishment of pax Americana in the area. Conversely, the USSR became interested in the area to prevent it from becoming a springboard for launching attacks against the Soviet mainland and later developed a vested interest in exploiting the Arab-Israeli and Arab-Western tensions to undermine Western positions militarily, politically and economically. Thus, the great-power struggle for dominant influence in the region was responsible for the escalation of regional tensions and conflicts. The interactions of local and external powers during the 1950s through the 1970s made the region one of the great tension areas of the world.

Soviet Policy in West Asia, 1945—1955

Soviet policy in a regional setting cannot be studied apart from its global setting at any given time. Both can be studied in terms of the basic conditioning factors of geography, economy, domestic political system, the ideology of the regime, and the international environment. These factors determine Soviet elite's perception of their national interests and their formulation of appropriate policies to promote them.[3]

The USSR played a limited role in international affairs during 1917-1945 as it was preoccupied with the consolidation of its domestic political base, transformation of its economy on socialist lines and massive armament for the defence cf the country.

World War II resulted in the relegation of the erstwhile European great powers to a secondary status in international politics and emergence of the USA and the USSR as the world-powers surpassing all others in terms of geographical size, natural resources, military potential and manpower. The post-war Soviet foreign policy bears the weight of this newly acquired status as a global or superpower.

The pivotal assumption in our discussion of Soviet policy and conduct is that it is motivated not by one but by a variety of factors in constantly shifting combinations. The widespread misconception about the ideological nature of Soviet policy was largely due to the long domination of a single leader (Joseph Stalin) in the USSR who was obsessed with the two-camp theory, the capitalist encirclement, the impossibility of co-existence with the Western world and the inevitability of coexistence with the Western world and the inevitability of war. The first indication of the fact that ideology was not the prime mover of Soviet policies came from the de-Stalinization campaign in 1956 and radical revision of the erstwhile Comintern approach towards the colonial world.[4]

The basic principles of post-Stalin foreign policy have been succinctly laid down in Article 28 of the 1977 constitution : "The foreign policy of the USSR is aimed at ensuring international conditions favourable for building communism in the USSR, safeguarding the state interests of the Soviet Union, consolidating the positions of world socialism, supporting the struggle of peoples for national liberation and social progress, preventing wars of aggression, achieving universal and complete disarmament, and consistently implementing the principle of the peaceful co-existence of states with different social systems."

These principles of Soviet Policy symbolize the compromise between the ideal and the real and provide an ideological basis for the pursuit of real Soviet national interests globally and regionally. The major preoccupations of Soviet policy during the 1970s were the pursuit of detente in bilateral relations with the USA, implying more active collaboration and co-operation with that country than was possible under a policy of peaceful co-existence in conditions of cold war : detente and collective security in Europe ; search for a *modus vivendi* with China ; avoidance of direct confrontation with the USA and prevention of the outbreak of nuclear war ; quest for superiority in conventional and strategic weapons ; and competitive peaceful co-existence with the USA in the open areas of the Third World. These interests and objectives also conditioned Soviet attitudes and policies towards the West Asian region, which cannot be understood other than in relation to the global balance of power and competition with the USA and China.

The Soviet Union's interest in West Asia is basically strategic-political (national security and quest for recognition as a regional power). Ideological and economic interests would seem to be subordinate to this primary interest. Located in the immediate vicinity of the USSR, the region has always attracted Tsarist and Soviet interest.

To the Tsarist regime is attributed a historic relentless search for outlets for its land-locked territory to the warm waters of the Mediterranean and the Indian Ocean. Russia sought the control of the Turkish straits to this end. During the nineteenth century Russian ambitions were thwarted by the rival European powers. Between the two World Wars, the Bolshevik regime remained aloof from the region due to the former's preoccupation with domestic problems and also to the preponderance of British and French influence in the region. The dogmatic approach of the Comintern towards the colonial areas was also not helpful. Nevertheless, the Bolshevik regime remained concerned till the early 1950s with its immmediate neighbours—Turkey, Iran and Afghanistan. Then prior to the outbreak of World War II, the traditional Russian interest was revived with the sinister understanding arrived at in 1939 between the Soviet Union and Nazi Germany to the effect that "the area south of Batum and Baku should be recognized as the main area of Soviet aspirations".[5]

During World War II, the survival of the Soviet state itself was at stake. Soviet interest in the area then was confined to this region's usefulness as a corridor through which supplies from the Western allies could be secured. In exercise of her right under the Treaty of Friendship with Iran, and in agreement with her War-time allies, the Soviet Union occupied the northern part of Iran till the termination of war. However, after the end of war, Soviet troops were not withdrawn and they installed a puppet communist regime in northern Irani province of Azerbaijan. It was only under heavy Western pressure and Iranian resistance that these forces were withdrawn.

At the end of World War II, the Soviets revived their territorial demands against Turkey which by remaining neutral during the War had earned the wrath and hostility of the Soviet leaders. They pressed for both strategic presence in the vicinity of the Straits and return of the territory ceded by Russia to Turkey at Brest-Litovsk. These demands were successfully resisted by Turkey and the Western powers.

The Arab-Jewish conflict and the Palestine question evinced the interest of Soviet leaders and provided them with an opportunity to move in. This time the Soviets backed the

Western-sponsored proposal for the partition of Palestine and the creation of an independent Jewish state. When the State of Israel was proclaimed in 1948 the Soviets accorded immediate *de jure* recognition and extended military and diplomatic support. The objective then was elimination of British influence from the area as well as consolidation of a progressive, pro-Soviet regime. But expectations went awry.

The great-power orientations of Soviet foreign policy became manifest when the Palestine question came before the UN General Assembly in 1947. It is curious to know why and how the Soviet Union championed the cause of world Zionism and became the god-parent of the Zionist state after pursuing a consistent policy of anti-Zionism from 1917 to 1946.

The Soviet attitude towards the Russian Jewry has been full of complexities and contradictions. It cannot be simply described as anti-Semitism : the Bolsheviks decried anti-Semitism and were opposed only to the Jewish bourgeoisie and Zionism and not to the Jews as an ethnic community. To Lenin, the idea of Jewish nationalism was a reactionary idea and inconsistent with the interests of the Jewish proletariat. Stalin's thesis against the Zionist movement (in *Marxism and the National Question*, 1913) was based on the premise that the Jews did not constitute a nation. Criticism of Jewish nationalism and Zionism as a reactionary ideology linked with the idea of national exclusivism and racial superiority has been a constant feature of Soviet propaganda. Yet Soviet solution to the Russian Jewish problem has varied from their attempted assimilation within the framework of the Soviet nationalities policy to a tacit recognition of their right to emigrate to Israel. (Emigration of East European Jews to Israel had started in 1948). A Jewish territorial home was established in 1928 in Birobidjan. In 1934 this territory was declared to be an autonomous region. Later, because of lack of enthusiasm among the Jews the experiment failed.

Immediately after World War II, the Soviet position on the Palestine question was just the opposite of the American position. After the War the Soviet Union supported the efforts of Arab countries for complete independence. At the United Nations the Soviet delegate supported the Syrian, Lebanese and Egyptian demands for the withdrawal of foreign forces from their territory. The formation of the Arab League in March 1945 was hailed as the first stage in the Arab national struggle for independence.[6] On Palestine, the Soviet position was explained by the noted Soviet Arabist V.B. Lutskiy in a public lecture delivered in Moscow in August 1946. He declared that a Palestine State ought to be an Arab state and that Zionism was utopian idea supported by certain Western powers in their own interest : The Palestine problem cannot be resolved by Imperialist means. "The majority of the population of Palestine regards the country as an Arab country and regards the Jews as citizens of an independent and democratic Arab Palestine."[7] He felt that the report of the Anglo-American Committee of Inquiry published in April 1946 failed to show that the Arab-Jewish conflict was a result of the British imperialist policy.

At the end of 1946 the Soviet position could be summed up in the following points : (i) any steps to deal with the Palestine question must be taken through the United Nations; (ii) the problem of European Jews must not be linked with the problem of Palestine ; (iii) withdrawal of Britain from Palestine was essential for a settlement, and (iv) Palestine ought to be an Arab state with Jews having equal civil rights. Soviet position remained unchanged till the beginning of 1947. The idea of partition was criticized as a programme to consolidate British strongholds in the area.

The Soviet support to the partition of Palestine in mid-1947 and the later Soviet-Israeli arms deal which decided the outcome of the Arab-Jewish war in 1948 in favour of the Jews cannot be explained except in geopolitical terms. When the Egyptian demand for the evacuation of the British armed forces from the Nile Valley and the Suez Canal Zone became more insistent and the February 1946 massive public demonstrations seemed to portend the things to come, rumours spread that the British planned a withdrawal from Egypt and estabilishment of Palestine as a rear base for the defence of the Suez Canal. Thus the fear of British entrenchment

ment in Palestine might have been one of the factors shaping Soviet policy. This threat could be avoided only by expelling the British from the country and by assuring Palestine's independence. Since a unitary bi-national state seemed to be impossible the Soviet leaders seized upon the idea of its partition into two independent Arab and Jewish states. Hence Soviet delegate Andrei Gromyko's open championship of the Zionist cause before the UN General Assembly on 14 May 1947.[8]

The widening gap between the Zionist movement and British policy in Palestine, the growing divergence of Jewish colonial interests from British imperial interests since 1939 and especially during World War II, the horrible experiences of European Jews during the War, the pro-Arab swing in British policy, and the apparently progressive character of the Jewish colonization of Palestine – all these factors seemed to incline the Soviet Union to adopt a pro-Zionist attitude.

The Soviet role first in getting the resolution on partition of Palestine through the UN General Assembly on 29 November 1947, then in consolidation of Israel when the Zionist State was proclaimed on 14 May 1948 by the supply of arms and diplomatic support is well chronicled.[9] The two most likely motives behind Stalin's volt-face have been suggested by Isaac Deutscher : (1) Inasmuch as Stalin was concerned with West Asia at that time, he considered Britian as the main enemy there. He supported the Partition Plan and later recognized the State of Israel and aided it with arms as the first step towards the elimination of British colonialism from the area. The independence of the area was an immediate aim, and the form of independence a secondary matter, and (2) since the Soviet-American Cold War at that time had reached to a stage when direct confrontation with the USA had become a distinct possibility and since the Soviet Union was still behind the USA in matter of nuclear arms it found that by supporting the American position on Palestine it was ameliorating the situation and lessening the danger of confrontation with America.

Another probable factor would have been Soviet over-estimation of the progressive character of Jewish nationalism and under estimation of the capability of the Arabs. They might have hoped that by supporting the progressive Jewish State amidst the sea of Arab backwardness and reaction they would be able to get a foothold in Palestine.

Ever since its accceptance of the recommendation of the United Nations Special Committee on Palestine on 13 October 1947 the Soviet Union stood immovably behind it. Together with the United States, it was largely responsible for raising a majority in the General Assembly on 29 November 1947 when Resolution 181 (II) was adopted by 33 votes to 13 with 10 abstentions along the still ill-defined lines of the UN Special Committee report. From the outbreak of war in Palestine on the proclamation of Israel till its end, the Soviets supported the Jews in Palestine both in arms and diplomacy. In this war the Soviet-approved Czechoslovak-Israeli arms deal was crucial, even decisive, for Israel's survival and victory.[11] The Soviets engaged in a cold war against the USA and Britain when they tried to establish some sort of an interim trusteeship in Palestine and opposed the plan. The USSR also condemned Arab invasion of Palestine and supported the American proposal for imposing sanctions against the invading Arab states, while the British delegate successfully opposed these sanctions. On 18 May, 1948, three days after the proclamation of Israel, the Soviet Union recognized it *de jure* while America accorded it mere *de facto* recognition. The Soviets established diplomatic relations with Israel in August when the Security Council in its last action before 14 May 1948 established a truce commission, from which the Soviet Union and the East European states were ingeniously kept out the Soviet delegate Gromyko, while generally supporting the idea of truce on 6 July, condemned the Report of the UN Mediator Count Folk Bernadotte and alleged that imperialist powers were trying to use the truce for a new deal on Palestine behind the back of the UN and in contravention of its earlier decision on partition of Palestine into Jewish and Arab states. When the General Assembly on 11 December, 1948 adopted Resolution 194 (III) creating a Conciliation Commission for Palestine to facilitate the rehabilitation of the refugees, the Soviet Union opposed the draft as it did not make a reference to withdrawal of all foreign troops from Palestine. According to Eytan, the

Armistice Agreements between the Arab states and Israel "could probably not have been concluded at all if the 'Cold War' in 1949 attained the proportions it attained since, specifically in the Middle East."[13] The Soviet delegate was the first to vote in favour of Israel's admission to the United Nations in November 1948. With active Soviet support, Israel was admitted to the world body on 4 March, 1949.[14]

The same strategic-political considerations which inclined the Soviet Union to become a party to the creation of Israel and its consolidation during 1948-49, became responsible for a shift in Soviet attiude and policy towards Israel by the autumn of 1949 which was marked by the exchange of sarcastic notes between Moscow and Tel Aviv.[15] The reason as stated in Soviet commentaries for the grudge against Israel were : its economic linkages with the USA ; the view that Zionism had become an ally of US imperialism ; the suspicion that she had aggressive intentions against her neighbours; her potentiality as a possible base against the Soviet Union; the view that the ruling elite in Israel was reactionary, pursuing class interests; and the charge that they had allowed the persecution of the Arab minority and discrimination against the Arab workers.[16] Israel's alliance with the West in the East-West Cold war was the main cause of Soviet indifference to Israel and gradual tilt towards the Arab states.

The change in Soviet tactics began in 1949 itself when the Soviet Union joined the Arab bloc in the UN and reaffirmed a resolution calling for the internationalization of Jerusalem.

A survey article in the *New Times*[17] dwelt on the question of Anglo-American rivalry in the region. It traced the recent history of this rivalry in a number of countries including Israel. The Palestine war (which in 1948 was described as Arab aggression on Israel) was now ascribed to intense intrigues and rivalry among the imperialists. For the first time, Israel was included among parties responsible for instigating this war.

In 1950 Israel's request for a guarantee on the part of western powers for the *status quo* in West Asia elicited a policy statement by the UK, the USA and France, which came to be known as the Tripartite Declaration, issued on 25 May, 1950.

Its object was threefold (i) stabilization of the Arab-Israel frontiers established under the Armistice Agreements of 1949 and opposition to their violation by any party; (ii) opposition to the development of an arms race between the Arab states and Israel; and (iii) defence of the area against the Soviet Union. The effect of the Tripartite Declaration was to remind the local states and the Soviet Union that the area was still in the Western security zone and that the West intended to be the custodian of its internal peace and its defender against foreign threats. 'Defence of the area as a whole' in the diplomatic language of the West meant defence against the Soviet Union. The Soviet Union, for its part, has always seen the Western plans for defence of West Asia as the beginning of aggression against itself. The Soviet reaction was prompt. The Soviets not only resented being left out of this agreement among the great powers regarding West Asia but also became alarmed about the military blocs in the region as a complement to the North Atlantic Treaty. Henceforth, the global East-West conflict was superimposed on the Arab-Israeli conflict.

Presumably in reaction to the Tripartite Declaration and the Israeli-American agreement of commerce and navigation in 1951 the Soviets began to shift their attitude towards Israel in the United Nations. In 1952, a draft resolution presented by eight countries calling for direct negotiation between the Arab states and Israel with a view to reaching a settlement of their outstanding differences (while at the same time activating the Conciliation Commission for any possible resumption of indirect negotiations) had passed the committee stage with the Soviet bloc abstaining. But in sympathy with Arab opposition to direct negotiations the Soviet bloc defeated the move by voting against it in the plenary meeting of the General Assembly.[19]

The nadir in Soviet-Israeli relations was reached when after a bomb explosion in the Soviet Chancery in Tel Aviv in February 1953, Moscow sent a strong protest note[20] to Israel and broke diplomatic relations, which were not resumed before July the same year.

In October the same year, the question of Israel's building

irrigation and hydroelectric projects in the Demilitarized Zone between Syria and Israel in contravention of the Armistice Agreement came for hearing. When an Anglo-French-American draft resolution favourable to Israel was presented on 21 January, 1954, the Soviet delegate insisted that Syria's consent was necessary for any project taking place in the Demilitarized Zone and that the Council should take no action until a bilateral agreement was reached. The next day, the Soviet Union exercised its negative vote against the draft, the first ever on a matter which did not concern any vital Soviet interest.[21] (The projects were illegally completed despite the Soviet veto).

In January 1954 Israel brought a complaint before the Security Council against Egypt's disregard of the 1951 Security Council Resolution calling Egyptian blockade of Israeli shipping through the Suez Canal as "inconsistent with the letter and spirit of the Egyptian—Israeli Armistice Agreement." Then, the Soviet Union had allowed the measure by abstaining from vote. But now a resolution calling for an end of the blockade by New Zealand and supported by the Western powers was vetoed by the Soviet Union.[22] Henceforth, every move in Soviet policy towards Israel was determined in the light of Soviet-Arab relations.

Up to 1956, the Arab East was regarded to be a Western sphere of influence by the Soviets and, according to Khrushchev, when King Farouk of Egypt once asked Stalin to give him arms with which he could force Britain to evacuate its troops from the Suez Canal Zone, he refused. "Stalin said in my presence that the Near East was part of Britain's sphere of influence and that therefore we couldn't go sticking our nose into Egypt's affairs."[23]

Soon after the Arab-Israeli war of 1948 the Arab world entered a period of turmoil and transition. Syria and Lebanon became independent and anti-British feeling ran high in Egypt and Iran. The rising tide of anti-imperialism in the third world in general, and the Arab East in particular, did provide many opportunities to the Soviets. However, they could not be exploited due to the rigid, doctrinaire Stalinist postures in foreign policy. For Stalin then the third world simply did not exist. There could be no middle ground between the camps of socialism and capitalism. But soon after the death of Stalin, the collective leadership, in a process of reassessment of the world situation and reformulation of their strategy, embarked upon major doctrinal revisions and necessary reorientations of policy. This process culminated in the proclamations of the Twentieth Congress of the Communist Party in 1956.

It was realized now that Asian nationalists were worth collaborating with against imperialism even if they were bourgeois and reactionary. National bourgeoisie was henceforth accepted as a "progressive" force and "national liberation" as a precondition of "social revolution".[24] Along with this general reorientation of attitudes towards the third world came the Soviet rapprochement with the Arabs caused by Soviet apprehensions about a possible encirclement of the Soviet Union through the ring of alliances of which the Baghdad Pact was one. The pro-Arab gestures were visible as early as 1950 when the Soviets gave full support to the Egyptian demand for the withdrawal of British forces from Egypt and Sudan. They assured Egypt that if she kept away from Western-sponsored defence pacts, her neutrality would be respected by the Soviet bloc and that the Soviet Union would provide military aid and training to build up the national defence forces.[25]

In 1951 the Soviet Union vetoed a resolution in the Security Council calling upon Egypt to end the blockade of the Gulf of Aqaba and ban on Israeli shipping through the Suez Canal.[26] During 1953-54 the Soviet Government abandoned its attitude of neutrality in the Arab-Israeli conflict and took a definitely pro-Arab stand.[27] At the United Nations, the Soviet delegation started giving moral and diplomatic support to the Arab causes. The first indication of Moscow's changed policy was made in the deliberations of the Security Council over Israeli invasion of the Gaza Strip during February 1955. The Soviet Government this time openly condemned the Israeli attack.

On 16 April 1955, just after Turkey and Iran had joined the Baghdad Pact, the Soviet Government issued a grim warning to the USA. It insisted that military blocs against the Soviet Union were unnecessary, that the Soviet Union had a special interest in the region and that it was close to the Soviet Union but thousands of miles away from the USA.[28] In it was also indicated that in view of the recent developments the Soviet Union had no choice but to win the non-committed Arab states to its side. To match the word with deed, it invited these countries to submit their requirements for aid and promised them sympathetic consideration.

This Statement was a landmark in the history of Soviet-Arab relations because, in addition to expressing Soviet concern over the anti-Soviet moves, it marked the official renunciation of a policy of indifference to and non-involvement in West Asian regional affairs.

The Soviet-Egyptian arms deal of 1955 and the Soviet-Syrian arms deal of 1956 were a tangible manifestation of this basic shift in Soviet attitude and policy.

From the Egyptian viewpoint, the Baghdad Pact, though formally directed against communism, was in fact a consolidation of the pro-Western forces in the region and posed a direct threat to the revolutionary nationalist regime in Egypt. Moreover, Iraq, the regional linchpin of the alliance, was a traditional rival of Egypt for the leadership of the Arab world. As Iraq's power and position rose with the Western aid so Egypt's influence seemed to decline correspondingly. Egypt countered this situation with pan-Arabism, non-alignment and close cooperation with the Soviet bloc. The threat from the growing Israeli military might and Egyptian weakness due to the Western embargo on arms was also one of the factors behind Egyptian acceptance of the Soviet offer of the arms aid.

In implementing their new strategy in the Arab world the Soviets employed a number of techniques and tactics : (i) by emphasizing the principle of peaceful coexistence of different social and political systems thereby allaying the fear of Arab states of internal communist subversion ; (ii) by identifying the Arab nationalist struggle with the anti-imperialist struggle of the Soviet bloc ; (iii) by providing generous and disinterested military/economic aid and diplomatic support ; and (iv) by concluding, during the 1970s, treaties of friendship and cooperation with a number of countries beginning with

Egypt in 1971 (abrogated in 1976), with Iraq in 1972 and Syria in 1980.

Reacting to the communique issued at the conclusion of Eisenhower-Eden conference in Washington on 1 February, 1956, the Soviet Foreign Ministry in its statement of 13 February warned against any Western intervention in the area under the Tripartite Declaration of 1950 and outside the UN framework. It was declared therein that "any action leading to complications in the Near and Middle East, and to increased tension in that area, is bound to be subject of legitimate concern on the part of the Soviet Government."[29] This was followed by still another statement on 18 April, 1956, regarding the situation in the area and the formation of military alliances "which is a source of international friction and conflicts and the cause of deterioration of relations between various states of the area." It was further declared that "the Soviet Union regarded as unlawful and impermissible, from the stand-point of universal peace, the attempts to make use of the Arab-Israeli conflict for intervention from outside in the domestic affairs of the independent Arab states or for introducing foreign troops into the territory of the Near East."[30]

Moscow's acute security interest was evinced by a series of Soviet reactions to a quick succession of events and crisis in West Asia following the Suez-Sinai crisis, the crisis in Lebanon, the crisis in Jordan, American intervention in the Lebanon, and the Iraqi revolution.[31]

Soviet strategic involvement in the area was accompanied during the 1960s by a major shift in Soviet strategic thinking in the wake of stationing in the Mediterranean first of American strategic aircraft carriers during the 1950s, then of the Polaris submarines directed against the Soviet industrial hinterland. Henceforth, a major Soviet objective became the building up of a Soviet naval presence in the Mediterranean with a view to eliminating the American Sixth Fleet from there or at least neutralizing it and blunting its political edge. As early as 1956, the Soviet Union had denounced American hegemony in the eastern Mediterranean. The strategic and economic dependence of the Soviet Union on the Mediterranean as the only round the year outlet via the Black Sea is an important determinant of Soviet policy. Other Soviet ports are icebound for most of the year. For the Soviet Union the Mediterranean is the gateway to the world at large, westward through the Straits of Gibralter and eastward through the Suez Canal. Hence the dictum that "the USSR is a Black Sea Power and, consequently, a Mediterranean Power" has the logic of geography behind it.

The beginning of the Soviet naval build-up in the Mediterranean during the 1960s reflected a new concern for acquiring strategic flexibility and mobility by developing and deploying conventional forces in aid of diplomacy. This was motivated not only by a desire to attain strategic parity with the USA but also by a positive desire of using the Mediterranean and the Suez Canal as a gateway to the Persian Gulf, Africa and the larger area around the Indian Ocean in search of influence and political gain.

The deployment of the Soviet Fifth Fleet in the Mediterranean represented a great change in Soviet military capability. During Khrushchev's time, the Soviet Union could not play an active role in the third world areas due to her inferiority to the USA in respect of strategic mobility and conventional sea and air power. Khrushchev, a product of the "massive retaliation" thinking, could not grasp the role of conventional forces in supporting and upholding diplomatic initiatives. The fuilure had been responsible for the Soviet retreat during the Cuban Missile Crisis of 1962. It was left to Khrushchev's successors to achieve parity with the USA in respect of strategic as well as conventional naval and air power. As a result, the threat posed to the security of the mainland USSR during the 1950s and 1960s has been eliminated.

The Soviets began the first sustained deployment of surface warships in the Mediterranean during 1964.[32] Moscow sought alternative Mediterranean bases when the Soviet navy's submarines stationed at Valona, Albania, were expelled by the Albanian Government in May 1961. It is noteworthy that Admiral Sergei Gorshkov paid his first visit to Egypt in December 1961 ostensibly with that purpose. Between March 1965 and February 1967 Gorshkov visited Egypt three more times. There were three ship-visits to Egyptian ports between

September 1965 and August 1966. His third visit occurred in May 1966, accompanying Prime Minister Alexei Kosygin, after which Egypt denied reports that it would concede base rights to the Soviets. The Soviet build-up was gradual but became considerable following the June 1967 War. Soviet ships were given access to Egyptian ports in July 1967. A five-year agreement for access to "facilities" (read "bases") was signed with Egypt in March 1968,[33] and Soviet warships were permitted the use of Port Said, Alexandira, Sollum and Mersa Matruh. Using these facilities Soviet aircraft engaged in reconnaisance and surveillance missions over the units of the American Sixth Fleet. Even after the expulsion of the Soviet military advisers from Egypt in July 1972, the Soviet ships continued to be allowed limited use of Egyptian naval facilities till President Anwar Sadat terminated them with his unilateral abrogation of the Soviet-Egyptian Friendship Treaty in 1976. It was in this year that the first Soviet aircraft carrier named *Kiev* entered the waters of the Mediterranean via the Turkish Straits, heralding Soviet naval parity with the USA and ending dependence on offshore or base facilities in the littoral states.

In the light of these developments, the relative strategic importance of the Mediterranean and the Arab East has declined. Now the locus of superpower rivalry has subtly shifted in the direction of the larger Indian Ocean area. The reopening of the Suez Canal greatly facilitated the build-up of a formidable Soviet naval presence in the Indian Ocean. But Soviet interest in the Afro-Asian seas is more than a strategic interest ; it also derives from the desire of the USSR as a global power to play a prominent role in regional affairs and develop a wide range of economic, political and military relations with the littoral states.

Since World War II the Soviet Union has insisted on the maximum exploitation of its status as a great power. Two trends have flowed from this principle : (i) the Soviet Union has always stressed and magnified the role of big-power consultations in maintaining peace ; and (ii) it has insisted on its recognition as a great power legitimately interested in the problems of the contiguous regions and having a right to participate in international deliberations over their affairs.

Soviet interest in the partition of Palestine, Soviet role during the Suez crisis, and Khrushchev's penchant for summit conferences on West Asia problems, are all illustrative of this interest. That concern was typically reiterated in the report of the Central Committee to the 24th Congress of the Communist Party of the Soviet Union in March 1971 : "Our country is prepared to join other powers who are permanent members of the Security Council, in providing international guarantees for a political settlement in the Middle East. Once this is reached, we feel that there could be a consideration of further steps designed for a military detente in the whole area, in particular, for converting the Mediterranean into a sea of peace and friendly cooperation."[34] There are innumerable examples of similar diplomatic initiatives from 1957 to 1977.

Although Khrushchev never recognized the idea of pan-Arab unity as a progressive one, it was left to his successors to grasp the anti-imperialist potential of this idea. The main Soviet ideological purpose in the Arab East since 1967 seems to consolidate a bloc of progressive Arab states firmly tied to the socialist bloc. The Soviets have been inclined not only to mould the Arab policies to Soviet requirements but also preferred that their social, economic and political structures approximate to the Soviet model. However, Moscow has seldom openly espoused the cause of proletarian revolution in this region or sided with the local communist parties in their contest for power with bourgeois regimes. The closer a country followed the Soviet road to development the more acceptable it became to the Soviet Union. Soviet foreign aid programmes have been directed towards strengthening the public sectors in the recipient countries. After the June 1967 War the Soviets openly exhorted Nasser to usher in a social revolution by purging the army and bureaucracy of bourgeois elements.

Soviet economic interest in West Asia is subordinate to its strategic-political interest. Although the Soviet Union is the world's largest producer and the fifth largest exporter of oil and has 1/3rd of the world's proven natural gas reserves, the growing needs of Soviet and East European industrial machines are likely to incline her to look towards the Arabian oil. Soviet oil policies in West Asia/North Africa have been conditioned by political as well as pragmatic economic considerations. As part of their overall drive to liquidate Western influence, the Soviet have encouraged the nationalization of foreign concerns and the use of oil as a political weapon against the West in the belief that the Western control over the oil resources of the area is the key to Western political and economic domination.

Soviet aim in this region seems to be both defensive and moderately expansionist in the sense of seeking influence in it, not Sovietizing it. The Soviets have sought to secure a firm and dependable beachhold from which to spread their influence to areas beyond. Hence their cultivation of Egypt and Syria. Thus, during the decade 1955—1964 they pursued aims in the region that were similar to those of Tsarist Russia. In the period 1965—1967 they sought to establish in Egypt and Syria a viable base for durable political influence. However, they found their advances countered by persistence of nationalist tendencies and by lack of such comprehensive geolinkages as existed between the Soviet Union and eastern Europe, putting severe constraints on Soviet ability to penetrate the area. The War of 1967 introduced new limitations on Soviet objectives. However valuable they were in Soviet eyes, the Soviets were not prepared to risk a direct confrontation with the USA for the Arab cause. Moscow was forced to reappraise her commitments to the Arabs and consequently formulated and implemented a short-term policy of redressal of military balance and a long-term policy of temporization with Arab-Israeli conflict, which eventually culminated in the Arab-Soviet discord. The stalemate of "no war, no peace" and Arab immobilism during 1968-1972 should be seen in light of this reappraisal of Soviet foreign policy under domestic and foreign pressures.

Inasmuch as the major foci of Soviet foreign policy during the 1970s were the detente with the USA, collective security in Europe and competition with China, the region became of low priority in Soviet calculations. The Arab-Israeli conflict had not only outlived its utility in furthering Soviet interests but entailed escalation of cost and risk and jeopardised Soviet regional and global interests. From 1973 onwards Moscow preferred a political settlement in the region with the Soviet Union as a co-guarantor with the other great powers. Such a settlement was likely to legitimize and formalize the Soviet role in the area. However, the Egyptian-Israeli Peace Treaty negated that expectation and the Soviet Union was relegated to the marginal countries in the area to continue her search for influence. During the early 1980s the Soviet Union continued to follow the post-detente stance of "measured neglect" towards the intra-regional criseis but appeared to be anxious to preserve its relationship with such friendly states which have preferred cooperation with it. In foreign affairs, one may conclude, the Soviet Union today appears to be a thoroughly conservative and nationally-oriented, rather than a radical-revolutionary and internationalist state.

REFERENCES

1. *The Middle East and North Africa* 1982-83 (London, 1983) ; S.H. Longrigg, *Oil in the Middle East* ; its discovery and development. 3rd ed. (London, 1978) ; Benjamin Shwadran, *The Middle East Oil and the Great Powers.* 3rd ed. (London, 1973) ; Leonard Mosley, *Power Play* : The Tumultuous World of Middle East Oil 1890-1973 (London, 1973).
2. See George E. Kirk, *Contemporary Arab Politics* : A Concise History (New York, 1961) ; Leonard Binder. *The Ideological Revolution in the Middle East* 2nd ed. (New York, 1982) ; Malcolm H. Kerr, *The Arab Cold War 1958-1970* : A Study of Ideology in Politics. 3rd ed. (London, 1972) ; Elizabeth Monroe, *Britain's Moment in the Middle East, 1914-1971.* 2nd ed. (Baltimore, 1981). Charles D. Cremeans, *The Arabs and the World* : Nasser's Arab Nationalist Policy (New York, 1963).
3. Cf. R.D. McLaurin, *The Middle East in Soviet Policy* (Toronto/ London, 1975), pp. 15-46 ; 47-66.
4. For the Comintern approach see Jane Degras, *The Communist International.* Documents. Vol. III (New York, 1960). pp. 530-541. For post-Stalin doctrinal revisions see Leo Gruliow, ed., *Current Soviet Policies.* Vol. II (New York, 1957) ; *Current Soviet Policies.* Vol. III (New York, 1960).
5. For a survey of Soviet attitudes towards the region during the inter-war period see Louis Fischer, *The Soviets in World Affairs 1917-1929.* 2 Volumes (Princeton, 1951) ; Ivor Spector, *The Soviet Union and the*

Muslim World, 1917-1957 (Seattle, 1959) ; Walter Z. Laqueur, *Communism and Nationalism in the Middle East* (London, 1956). For the Soviet interest in the Persian Gulf area see Sir Anthony Eden, *Memoirs* : Full Circle (London, 1960), pp. 357-58.

6. K. Serezhin, "The Problem of the Arab East". *New Times* (3) January 1949.
7. V. Lutskiy, "Palestinskaya Problems" (The Problem of Palestine). Moscow, 1946 A.R.C. Bolton, *Soviet Middle Eastern Studies.* Part IV (London, 1959), pp. 4-5 ; Z. Ben-Shlomo, "Soviets and Zionism". *Wiener Library Bulletin* 20 (Winter 1965-66).
8. UN General Assembly, *Official Record.* Special Session of the General Assembly (1947) 77th Plenary Meeting, pp. 127-135. (Hereinafter referred to as *GAOR*).
9. The Soviet position on partition of Palestine was made clear in the statement given by Gromyko before the General Assembly on 26 November, 1947 : *GAOR* 2nd Session, 125th Meeting, 26 November 1947, pp. 1358-1363. Cf. J.C. Hurewitz, *The Struggle for Palestine* (New York, 1950), pp. 288-289 ; Arnold Krammer, "Soviet Motives in the partition of Palestine, 1947-48". *Journal of Palestine Studies* 2 (Winter 1973) ; and Kermit Roosevelt, "The Partition of Palestine; A Lesson in Pressure Politics". *Middle East Journal* 2 (1), January 1948, pp. 1-16.
10. Isaac Deutscher, *Stalin* : *Political Biography*, London, 1965, pp. 591-93.
11. Golda Meir, *My Life* (London, 1975) p. 188, Jon Kimche and David Kimche, *Both Sides of the Hill* (London, 1960) p. 205.
12. Walter Eytan, *The First Ten Years* New York, 1958, p. 20.
13. *Ibid* , p. 46.
14. *Ibid.*, pp. 14-15 ; see also Jacob Malik's speech on 13 April, 1949 ; *GAOR* 3rd Session, Part II, 191st Plenary Mtg. 13 April 1949, pp. 45-46.
15. *Documents on International Affairs, 1949-50* (London, 1954).
16. Bolton, *Soviet Middle Eastern Studies* Part VI, p. iv ; Walter Z. Laqueur, *The Soviet Union and the Middle East* (London, 1959), pp. 148-49.
17. *New Times* (9), March 1950, pp. 3-9.
18. J.C. Hurewitz ed., *Diplomacy in the Near and Middle East*, Vol. II (Princeton, 1956), p. 308.
19. *GAOR*, 7th Session, Ad Hoc Political Committee, 39th Mtg., 11 December 1952 ; *Ibid.*, 7th Session, 405th Plen. Mtg. 18 December 1952.
20. Text in *Middle Eastern Affairs* 4 (April 1953), p. 131.
21. UN Security Council, *Official Record.* 655 Mtg., 21 January 1954. (Hereinafter referred to as *SCOR*).
22. *SCOR*, 664th Mtg. 29 March, 1954.
23. Strobe Talbott, *Khrushchev Remembers* (London, 1971), p. 436.
24. Gruliow, ed., (*note* 4).

25. John Connel, *The Most Important Country* (London, 1957). p. 23.
26. Coral Bell, *Survey of International Affairs*, 1954 (London, 1957), p. 217.
27. John C. Campbell, *Defence of the Middle East* (New York, 1958), 217.
28. *Documents on International Affairs*, 1955 (London, 1959), pp. 300-304.
29. *Documents on International Affairs*, 1956 (London, 1960), pp. 53-56.
30. *Ibid.*, pp. 59-61.
31. *Cf. Documents on International Affairs*, 1957.
32. Michael MccGwire, ed., *Soviet Naval Developments* (New York, 1973), pp. 345 ff. See also David Fairchild, *Russia Looks to the Sea* : A study of the Expansion of Soviet Maritime Power (London, 1971).
33. As revealed in President Sadat's speech ; Radio Cairo, 3 April 1974/ BBC *Summary of World Broadcasts*/Part IV (Hereinafter referred as SWB/IV) ; Mohamed Heikal, *The Road to Ramadan* (London, 1975), pp. 47 ff.
34. *Keesing's Contemporary Archives*. 18 (1971-72), p. 24655.
35. See A.J. Berry, "Oil and Soviet Policy in the Middle East", *Middle East Journal* 26 (2), Spring 1972.

CHAPTER III

Forward Policy 1956-1966

The Suez Crisis

A close look at the factors and forces which were responsible for the Suez-Sinai Crisis of 1956 is indispensable to comprehend the underlying motives of Soviet diplomacy and its significance. While Arab-Western, Arab-Israeli, inter-Arab and East-West tensions were some of the focal points in the wider perspective, the Baghdad Pact, Israeli expansionism, the Soviet-Egyptian arms deal, and the withdrawal of the American offer of aid for the construction of the Aswan Dam were the immediate factors leading to the Suez crisis.[1]

The Arab struggle against Western imperialism was intensified after World War II.[2] After World War I, Britain and France were mandated to rule over the countries of the Arab East directly or indirectly. Britain which already controlled the Nile Valley, the Persian Gulf and South Arabia became the paramount power and the "guardian" of the area. The imperial powers not only dominated the region politically but also established their military bases there, exploited its economic resources, and above all, Balkanized it by creating divisions among its people on grounds of class and interest. family and clan, religion and sect and region.

Egypt, due to its central position in and its intellectual leadership of the Arab-world, is the most important country in the area. Britain was still in the early fifties the most important of the outside powers which had a wide range of interests in the area and well-entrenched there. With the revolution of July 1952 the Egyptian national movement entered a radical phase. The exigencies of the Cold War, the weakened position of Britain, and American pressure on Britain to evacuate its troops from Egypt and mend her relations with Egypt were responsible for the Anglo-Egyptian Treaty of 1953 under which Britain agreed to leave Sudan and the Anglo-Egyptian Treaty of 1954 under which British forces withdrew from the Suez Canal Zone. However, the hopes of establishing good relations with Britain vanished the next year when the Western efforts at organizing an anti-Soviet alliance in the area culminated in the signing of the Baghdad Pact.

Up to 1954, West Asia was considered to be a preserve of the Western powers. The early Cold War encounters with the USSR in Europe and Asia had impressed upon the Western powers the need for organizing this vulnerable area against a possible Soviet encroachment. However, the abortive Middle East Defence Organization plan of 1951[3] and the like to establish some form of regional arrangement were rubuffed by the Arab states, due to their suspicion of the Western motives as well as their experience with imperialism for decades. They had nothing to fear initially from the Soviet Union which did not have a record of imperialism in the area and which had not done them any wrong. They were more concerned with the menace of Israel than the imaginary danger of Soviet expansion. The Arab suspected that the Western schemes were just a cover for the return of imperialism.

However, the Western powers disappointed with the Arab countries had, sometime before the signing of the Anglo-Egyptian Agreement of 1954, begun to work upon a different project, namely, a military grouping of the countries situated in the immediate vicinity of the Soviet Union—Turkey, Iran and Pakistan. While announcing this "Northern Tier" plan, its progenitor, the US Secretary of State, John Foster Dulles admitted of the prevailing neutralist mood in some Arab countries and of the futility of enlisting their support for any regional arrangements.[4] Then the British, desirous of preserving their position in the Arab world and extending their and their allies' influence, manoeuvred for the inclusion of their client Arab states, Iraq and Jordan, in the proposed organization. The negotiations for such an alliance reached a decisive phase on 12 January, 1955 when it was announced that Turkey and Iran were shortly to conclude a defence pact,[5] with the participation, if possible, of other interested countries. Turkey had already been allied with Pakistan in 1954. Now the Baghdad Pact had two immediate repercussions. Firstly, it impinged heavily on the delicate balance of Arab politics. Apparently designed to contain the Soviet threat, the Pact was seen by the nationalists as an instrument of enhancing the prestige of Britain and Iraq in the Arab world.[6] It was a reaffirmation of the resolve by Western powers to maintain bases in the area. Therefore, it provoked sharp reactions from Egypt, a country aspiring for the political leadership of the Arabs. The ensuing cold war between the Arab states created great misunderstanding, mistrust and hatred between Egypt and England. By this time Egypt's non-alignment was confirmed with Nasser attending the Bandung Conference of the Afro-Asian nations in 1955.[8]

Secondly, the Baghdad Pact aroused the suspicions of the Soviet Union and sharpened her strategic interest in the area. The Soviets sharply reacted to the extension of NATO along its southern flank and took it as a grave threat to its security. It not only protested against the Pact but rushed to befriend the nationalist regimes which were opposed to the Pact for their own reasons.

After the termination under the Anglo-Egyptian Treaty of 1954 of British military presence in the Canal Zone where it had been since 1882, Egypt became the sole defender of the Suez Canal and the Sinai. Henceforth, frontiers with Israel became the main source of tension. In 1954 an Israeli ship *Bat Galim* which tried to break the Egyptian blockade was captured and impounded. In general, Arab-Israeli relations during the two years prior to the Suez crisis were characterized by rising tension on the border. The Israeli raid on 18 February, 1955 on the Egyptian garrison on the Gaza Strip in retaliation of a guerilla attack inside Israel, proved a decisive event in Egypt-Israel relations. This Israeli raid inflicted upon the Egyptians five times as many casualties as compared with the previous raid. This raid exposed the vulnerability of Egypt and required her to secure modern arms is sufficient quantities to overcome her weakness in relation to Israel.

Meanwhile, France, a signatory of the Tripartite Declaration was secretly arming Israel and thus making a mockery of the Western policy of maintaining an arms balance in West Asia.

Another development contributing to tension was the tightening of the Egyptian blockade of the Gulf of Aqaba. In retaliation, David Ben-Gurion, Prime-Minister-designate of Israel sent troops to occupy the El-Auja triangle on 21 September in preparation for the coming Sinai campaign. He also declared on 25 September that the Gulf would be opened to Israeli shipping in one year or less.[11] With this he created an atmosphere of crisis in which Egypt became quite alarmed about Israeli designs. Israeli forces were being rapidly modernized as a result of Franco-Israeli arms deal of 1954 (another was concluded in November 1955). Hence search for arms became the most urgent objective of Egyptian foreign policy to combat both the Baghdad Pact and Israeli designs. In September came the "Czech-Egyptian" arms deal, which had secretly been concluded with the Soviets after Egypt's efforts to purchase arms in Washington and London failed.

As Pierre Rondot has put it "the West held the Arab nation on a leash and sought to ignore its restlessness. So the Arab nation gave itself to the Russians who had noted its desires and promised to assuage them."[12] The arms deal was by far "the most unmistakable manifestation that a turning-point had been reached in Moscow's policy towards the area.[13] It was preceded by a general reorientation of Soviet attitudes and policy and a diplomatic offensive marked by Soviet Foreign Minister, Dimitriy Shepilov's tour of West Asia in the summer of 1955.[14]

Thus, the convergence in mid-fifties of the Soviet-Egyptian objectives against the Baghdad Pact and their united front to oppose the West led to the arms deal which allowed the USSR, in a single move, "to leap-frog" over the Northern Tier and became for the first time in its history, an effective West Asian power.[15]

The arms deal was a political move primarily directed against the West. It had nothing to do with the Arab-Israeli conflict or inter-Arab conflicts which were to her merely side issues. At this time the Soviets did not wish to get entangled with regional disputes. However, arms deliveries to Egypt had a direct bearing on the Arab-Israeli sector in particular, and the political situation in the area, in general. Tension continued to increase and the Soviet Union gradually became involved in the Arab-Israeli confrontation as well as in other local disputes.

Thus, the arms deal was to become one of the causes of the Suez crisis five months later. It shocked the Western powers greatly. "The United States", wrote Eisenhower, "could no longer remain a silent partner. We had to step in to counter the weight of Soviet power."[16] It was taken by Israel as a challenge to its supremacy and an obstacle to its designs and therefore decided to launch a "preventive" war against Egypt before any radical shift in the regional balance of power took place.

By this time the stage was being set for the coming crisis. The occasion which united Britain, France and Israel for action against Egypt was provided by the nationalization of the Suez Canal Company. The immediate cause of the latter act was the cancellation of the offer of aid for the construction of the Aswan High Dam by John Foster Dulles.

Egypt's economic development constituted an essential objective of Egyptian foreign policy, besides non-alignment, Arab nationalism and pan-Africanism. The construction of a dam on the Nile north of Aswan was a cherished dream of the revolutionary leadership ever since it came to power.[17] As soon as the news of the arms deal were made public Americans became anxious to prevent the deliveries and offset Soviet gains. The Aswan aid offer was meant to wean Nasser away from the Soviets and deny them the chance of financing this project.[18] The offer had a political rather than an economic reason and had been endorsed at the NATO Conference in December 1955, because the Soviets had in the previous year hinted at the possibility of Soviet aid.[19] This would have given them an opportunity for penetration of the area. But no sooner the Americans offered their assistance along with British and the World Bank, than the Soviet Ambassador in Cairo announced that the Soviet Union hoped it would be able to participate in the financing of the dam, "unless contrary stipulations in Egypt's accord with the Western powers exclude us specifically."[20] The Americans announced that they would never allow the Russians to join in. The Egyptians saw through the political and economic strings attached with Western offers and therefore bargained for more favourable terms.

But of late Nasser's radical anti-Western moves such as diplomatic recognition of People's Republic of China in May 1956 had antagonized the Western powers. In their view the aid offer had done nothing to arrest the growth of Soviet influence which was the underlying purpose. As a rebuff Dulles announced the withdrawal of the aid offer.

Soviet Reaction

In a speech at Alexandria on 26 July during the course of which he announced the takeover of the Canal, Nasser complained about Western treatment of Egyptian and Arab nationalism, their ignorance of the needs and demands of the Arabs and bitterly criticized Western reactions to the Arms Deal and the conditions attached to development aid.[21] The Canal was taken over as it was an Egyptian property. Its nationalization was also motivated by the desire to thwart a probable extension of the Company's concession or imposition of some sort of international control of Egypt.[22] Nasser later told Anthony Nutting that the purpose of his dramatic reaction had been to show that Egypt was not going to be pushed around by the West either on the Canal issue or the settlement with Israel.[23]

Britain still enjoyed dominant influence in the area. The British were not prepared yet to part with their imperial legacy. They reacted sharply to this challenge to their authority. As a *Times* editorial put it "... If Nasser is allowed to get away with his *coup* all the British and other Western interests in the Middle East will crumble ..."[24] Britain announced that nationalization contravened international agreements and guarantees and was therefore illegal and revocable. Eden records: "The Government determined that our essential interests in this area must be safeguarded, if necessary by military action, and that the needful preparations must be made ..."[25] "No arrangement for the future of this great international waterway could be accepted by Her Majesty's Government which could leave it in the unfettered control of a single pewer which could ... exploit it purely for purpose of national policy."[26] Britain's Prime Minister, Sir Anthony Eden, personally regarded Nasser as another Hitler.[27]

The seeds of the Suez Crisis thus lay in the decade of Anglo-Egyptian rivalry which reached its climax over the Baghdad Pact, and as Seale has put it, Britain attacked Egypt not because of the act of nationalization but "because the tide of his [Nasser's] influence in Arab-Asia threatened to engulf Jordan, Iraq, and the Gulf, together with British treaties, strong points, and oil interests."[28]

Like Britain, France too was deeply attached to the Suez Canal which was something of a symbol of its prestige in the area. Because of his support to Algerian rebels the French too were his enemies and suffered from the Munich complex.[29] Thus coincidence of the objectives of Britain, France and Israel was responsible for their collusion against Egypt. The French suggested the most effective way to strike at Egypt was through Israel whom they had been arming since 1954.[30]

According to Robertson, the origins of the Suez Crisis lay really in Israel where the decision to fight a "preventive" war was deliberately timed to take advantage of wide-spread disenchantment in Britain and France against Nasser.[31] To further their national aim, Israelis successfully exploited the emotions of the leaders of the two great powers and implicated them in their war of aggression. According to Childers, "the motives behind this aim were, as always, a fluctuating combination of religious-historical dreams, strategic designs, political necessity, and self-defence."[32] For achieving this protective-expansionist aim, advance planning had been undertaken.[33] They also wished to prevent the emergence of any militant and assertive leadership among Arabs.

American reaction to the act of nationalization was non-violent as compared to that of Britain and France. According to Cremeans, "The American reaction was indeed quite different from that of its British and French allies although the fact was not always apparent. Whereas they both soon referred to the possibility of using force, the American government never did so."[34] The initial pronouncement of the State Department did refer to the "seizure" of the Suez Canal but it indicated that the matter was one of concern mainly to the principal users of the Canal. The Americans were opposed to the use of force to resolve this problem since the very beginning.[35] Dulles emphasized the utilization of all possibilities of deliberation, conference, negotiation and recourse to the United Nations[36] and to avoid force altogether.[37]

From the very beginning the Franco-British approach diverged from the American. At his first meeting with the foreign ministers of France and Britain in London on 1 August, Dulles opposed force and recommended convening of an international conference.[38] The statement issued on 2 August after this tripartite conference condemned the act of nationalization in strong terms and proposed the establishment of "operating arrangements under an international system" consistent with legitimate interests of Egypt. A conference of the countries which were signatories of the Convention of 1888 was subsequently called in London. Then, significantly, Eden announced the same day that by "operating arrangements under an international system" Britain meant an "international authority" to manage the Canal's affairs.[39] The French premier also declared the same day that the proposed authority would have to control the day-to-day workings of the Canal. Hence on, American and Anglo-French positions were set at odds at every step till when the tripartite aggression took place America had to stop it.

The immediate Soviet reaction to the news of the nationalization was favourable to Egypt. The Soviet press congratulated Egypt on having at last become the master of the Canal[40] and affirmed that it rightfully belonged to Egypt. Open Soviet support of the Egyptians came on 31 July when Khrushchev publicly applauded the takeover of the Canal and declared that the action was completely legal.[41]

It has often been alleged that the Egyptian action was inspired by the Soviets. However, till now no reliable evidence has come into light which proves it. Nasser seemed to have acted on his own. The Soviets, though unembarrassed, were initially undecided and defended Egypt verbally. From this point onwards, all Soviet utterances and actions were marked by circumspection and caution. They were guided not by a crusading zeal for the sake of the Egyptians but by their own strategy of peaceful competition with the West, and their aspiration for being recognized as a regional power. They appeared to be aware of the dangers from a military involvement in the crisis. The Soviets, moreover, seemed to be mindful of the Western interests and in April last the statement issued after the conclusion of talks between Soviet Premier N.A. Bulganin and British Premier Eden, was conspicuous by full Soviet understanding of the Western position in the region.[42] In June 1955 during his Cairo visit Shepilov had categorically stated that the Soviet Union did not want to come between Egypt and the West and that it did not favour an Egyptian-Israeli war which would gain nothing for the Arabs. It might rather "trigger a third world war".[43]

The immediate reactions of the principal powers to the act of nationalization expressed, the course of the Suez crisis hence can be divided into two distinct phases : (i) the diplomatic phase marked by intense negotiations within international conferences and at the United Nations, and (2) the military phase marked by the Israeli invasion of the Sinai and Anglo-French intervention.

Soviet Policy During the Diplomatic Phase

The first London Conference of the maritime powers using the Suez Canal was convened by the United Kingdom in pursuance of the tripartite statement of August. A number of selected countries including Egypt and the Soviet Union were invited. Egypt boycotted the Conference calling it a "conference of aggression" but the Soviets agreed to attend though with some reservations. The express purpose of the conference was to get the principles contained in the tripartite statement endorsed by the majority of participants.[44] But covert Anglo-French motive seemed to gain time for preparation for armed intervention in Egypt.

The proceedings of the conference were opened by the American Secretary of States Dulles in a speech elaborating the three-power conclusions. These were embodied later in a draft plan presented to the conference on 20 August. This became known as the "Dulles plan" for internationalization of the Suez Canal.

In opposition to the Western proposals, the Soviet delegation presented on 23 August a draft communique[45] to be adopted by the conference, which called for negotiation of a Suez settlement "solely by peaceful means" through a committee including the United States, Britain, France, India and the USSR. This communique if adopted, would have barred the use of force by Britain and France in the event negotiations failed. The draft was not put for voting on procedural grounds.

Failing in this the Soviet delegation favoured the alternative Indian plan,[46] presented by Krishna Menon, which called for an international advisory board, and a new version of the convention which Egypt would be required to sign and which would be made subject to UN sanctions. It did not infringe Egypt's sovereignty and at the same time protected the interests of the user states. But this plan did not get the support of the majority.

The Anglo-American proposals were finally approved by a majority of 18 out of 22 participating powers and it was decided to send a committee of five under the Chairmanship of the Australian Prime Minister Robert Menzies to present and explain these proposals to Nasser in Cairo and ask him to negotiate on their basis.

The Committee began its meeting with Nasser on 4

September and had three sessions up to 6 September. But the mission ended in failure on 9 September when Nasser issued a statement in reply, declaring adherence to the 1888 Convention with its clauses about the freedom of passage, and proposed an international conference to discuss the problems. In other words, he accepted the solution of the eighteen powers so far as their five principles were concerned. These were : respect for the sovereign rights of Egypt ; guarantee of freedom of passage through the Canal according to the 1888 Convention ; respect for Egypt's right of ownership ; ensurance of efficient and dependable operation ; and the importance of maintenance and development of the Canal. Nasser refused to swallow the bait of the international managing board.

The Soviet Union, unlike Egypt, did not boycott the conference. It was for the first time that it was invited to an international conference on West Asian affairs. On 9 August the Soviets issued a statement[47] in reply to the tripartite statement of 2 August and the invitation to the London conference. It was a lengthy statement remarkable for its legalistic structure and well-reasoned arguments. It took exception to the composition, place and timing of the conference. It expressed Soviet disagreement with the principles and purposes of the three-power statement. It upheld the legality of the Egyptian action and denied that there was any connection between the act of nationalization and freedom of navigation through the Canal. The Western powers could object to nationalization only if Cairo refused to reimburse the Company's shareholders or interfered with the freedom of navigation in violation of 1888 Convention. The reasons for Western dissatisfaction and alarm were political rather than legal. Fearful of losing their influence in the Arab East, the United States, Britain and France had applied economic sanctions against Egypt and staged a display of force in the Eastern Mediterranean. These actions and summoning of the London conference were in violation of the Charter of the United Nations.

Referring to the military movements by Britain and France it said that the Soviet government considered these measures as a challenge to peace.

In addition it made a number of reservations regarding the

Soviet attitude, namely, that (i) the London Conference could not be regarded as an international meeting authorized to take any decisions on the Suez Canal, (ii) Soviet participation in the conference would not commit the USSR to any of the "obligation" set out in the three-power statement, or any which might infringe Egypt's right to nationalize the canal, (iii) invitations should have been extended to 22 more nations including the East European states, the Arab states, and People's Republic of China, and (iv) the conference should have been postponed until the end of August so that better arrangements could have been made.

Lastly, it declared that "the government of the Soviet Union is a determined supporter of further relaxation of international tension, including tension in the area of Near and Middle East. It is convinced that respect for sovereign rights of nations and the promotion of international cooperation in keeping with the spirit of the times, on the basis of equality and non-interference in the domestic affairs of nations, is the supreme condition for strengthening international confidence and ensuring lasting peace between the peoples."

When the conference started on 16 August the Soviet delegation led by Shepilov defended the Egyptian rights and opposed imperialist machinations. Although the Soviet delegation failed to get its own proposals or the Indian plan accepted by the conference, the Soviets gained in the goodwill of the Arab and Afro-Asian countries.

On the opening day of the Conference Shepilov made a speech[48] which largely recapitualted the arguments contained in the Soviet reply of 9 August.

In his speech the following day [49] he supported the Egyptian government's proposal for a wider international conference with the participation of states signatory to the 1888 Convention and of all states which make use of the Canal. He emphasized the necessity to settle the dispute by peaceful means and through negotiations.

But if Eisenhower is to be believed, Shepilov, while publicly supporting the Egyptian position, made it known to Dulles in private conversations that the Soviets were willing "to negotiate some kind of matually satisfactory arrangement with the

United States. The impression he tried to give was that the Soviets would be agreeable to imposing international controls upon Egypt, provided that the plan was so devised and worked as not to alienate the Arabs from the Soviets."[50] Shepilov also hinted that whatever was decided should bear the appearance of a joint Soviet-American action. Eden has noted that "the Soviet Government recognized our special interests in the Middle East," and that the Russians may not have forgotten there conversations of last year in London on the region. "The Russians may also have remembered that not many years before, during negotiations over the passage from the Black Sea to the Aegean, they had demanded international control of Suez."[51]

Notwithstanding this behind-the-scene activity, Soviet actions were aimed primarily at furthering its own interests. On the one hand the Soviets were bent on securing Western recognition of their position as a West-Asian power, and on the other hand, they wanted to impress upon the Afro-Asian world that they were the sincere champions of their cause. To this end, Moscow used the first London Conference as an international forum to blast the "atavistic colonial practices" of the Western powers.

Anti-imperialism was the dominant theme of Shepilov's subsequent statements. On 21 August he led a frontal attack on the Dulles plan declaring that the draft was incompatible with the sovereign rights of Egypt to the Suez Canal. Its purpose was to remove the Canal from the sovereignty, ownership and operation of Egypt, which is the mistress of the Canal. He called fcr condemnation of this "disruptive plan." Then he laid down his own principles for settlement which included international cooperation by setting up a consultation commission.

On 23 August, the last day of the Conference, when the American and Indian drafts were put to vote, Soviet delegation did not submit a draft of its own and supported the Indian plan, as according to it, this met the interest of their work.

As regards the 18-Power proposals, Shepilov charged that "As the group of countries putting forward these conditions, which are obviously inequitable and unacceptable to Egypt, apparently want Egypt's refusal of these ultimatum conditions to provide the pretext for accusing Egypt of being intransigent and unwilling to cooperate, and to leave their hands free for further action, it is perfectly clear that this line leads to the aggravation of the conflict."[52] He denounced the plan as designed to reimpose colonial control of Egypt.

Further, both the Indian and the Soviet delegations challenged the competence of the conference to pass a decision. The Conference was not composed on the principle of universality of membership, like the United Nations. It was a selected group with self-assumed authority. Shepilov demanded that the Conference be considered as only of "preliminary nature."

On 24 August again Shepilov told a press Conference in London that American plan "was based on an unacceptable colonialist position," and highlighted the Soviet approach "by means of ultimatums and threats to use force, is the colonialist way of solving the problems."[53]

On 26 August *Pravda* editorially warned the supporters of a "position of strength" settlement of the Suez question that "such action can entail serious international complications." At a diplomatic party on 27 August in Moscow, Khrushchev told the British and French ambassadors that if war broke out over Suez the Arabs would not stand alone. "It will be a just war for the Arabs, and there will be volunteers."[54]

On 14 September, the Soviet government accepted the suggestions made in Egyptian government's note given to other countries on 10 September, calling for an international conference to revise the 1888 Convention.

On 12 September, a letter from Soviet Premier Bulganin was sent to both Britain and France in which he denied reports that the Soviet government were inciting Egypt. Far from it, he maintained, the Soviet Union was eager to contribute to a peaceful settlement with due regard to the interests of all the states concerned. Nevertheless, the Soviets stood by Egypt. How could the Soviet Union, Bulganin asked, not treat favourably Egypt's position when she was defending her sovereignty and her national territory ? He then accused Britain and France of threatening Egypt's inalienable rights with the use of force and spoke of official declarations of the readiness of

Britain and France, on the pretext of defending their interests, to land their forces on the Egyptian territory and infring Egypt's territorial integrity and inviolability. He was aware, he said, that the two powers had stationed troops on Cyprus and that the Soviet Union could not stand aside if there were an invasion of Egypt. There was a danger that small wars can turn into big wars.[55]

Having failed to impose upon Egypt the 18-Power proposals by means of diplomatic pressure, Dulles brought out a second plan for internationalization of the Canal, that is, by the establishment of a "Suez Canal Users' Association" (SCUA) pending the final solution of the conflict. He recommended this scheme to Britain and France as an extension of the 18-Power proposals and the attendant formula for a settlement. The body was meant to be a device for collective bargaining with Nasser,[56] for mobilizing world public opinion, and for mutual assistance if the Suez Canal or the pipelines became blocked. Through this project Dulles was able to persuade his restive allies to postpone their plans for an immediate use of force. He wanted to gain time in the belief that anything was preferable to an outbreak of hostilities which, in his view, would only have served the purpose of the Soviet Union.

The occasion of the second London Conference of eighteen powers called to approve the SCUA scheme too was marked by a contrast of British and American approaches. On 13 September while announcing the SCUA plan, Dulles while answering questions afterwards, made a significant remark: "We do not intend", he said, "to shoot our way through. It may be we have the right to do it but we don't intend to do it as far as the United States is concerned." On the contrary, Eden thought that if Egypt refused to cooperate with the SCUA the Allies would be entitled to intervene. While announcing the scheme in Parliament he implied that it would, if need be, be backed by force.[57]

On the opening day of the conference Dulles explained that the purpose of the Association was not to enable "any one or more of us to impose our views upon any of our associates," still less "to coerce Egypt", and that the membership in the association would not involve the assumption by any member of any obligation.[58] Subsequently, he declared that so far as his own government was concerned, there was no intention "to impose by force the services offered to Egypt."

The Anglo-American differences of fundamental nature about the means and ends paralysed the SCUA plan before it could be put into operation. The deliberations of the second conference were marked by confusion and it ended indecisively calling for a third conference in London to draw up precise rules of the organization to open on 1 October.[59]

The outcome of Conference from Angio-French viewpoint, was at best "indifferent."[60] Anxious to end the argument, Eden and Guy Mollet decided on 22 September to refer the matter to the Security Council which decided on 26 September to discuss the matter on 5 October.

Meanwhile, a third conference met in London on 1 October to establish the machinery of the SCUA. An executive agency was set up. But its aims were still not clear. Dulles did not attend the meeting. He almost disowned the whole project because of Anglo-French arbitrariness. He pointed out the bnsic difference of approach and declared that America could not be expected to identify itself 100 per cent either with colonial powers or with the powers seeking independence. Referring to the SCUA he said that though there was now "talk about teeth being pulled out of the plan", there were never any "teeth in it, so far as I am aware."[61]

The Soviet Union, which along with other dissenters of the first conferences—India, Ceylon and Indonesia—had been excluded from the second conference, promptly protested against this. In a lengthy statement issued on 15 September the Soviet government asserted that "the USSR as a great power", was unable to "stand aloof," since "any violation of peace in the region of the Near and Middle East" could not "but affect the interests and security of the Soviet state."[62]

It took strong note of the continued threats to use force against Egypt made by Britain and France and the concentration of Anglo-French forces and fleets in the immediate vicinity of Egypt and declared that "This, undoubtedly, leads to a still greater aggravation of the situation in connection with the Suez Canal, and creates a position that is dangerous to peace." Moreover, it described the SCUA as a "dangerous provocation, leading to still greater aggravation of the situation in connection with the Suez question and to the artificial creation of incidents which could be used as a peitext for the use of force against Egypt." It also noted that the recall of foreign pilots working on the Canal was meant to disrupt the normal working of the Canal.

A commentary published in *Izvestia* on 20 September attacked the Dulles' scheme that in the event of Egyptian non-recognition of the SCUA its members boycott the Canal, as the "paralyzation plan". This was not prompted by disinterested considerations but by selfish motives originating with American monopolies.[63] Another commentary by *Pravda* on 22 September described the Association as an "imperialist plot" designed to apply political and economic pressure on Egypt.

In addition to moral and political support, the USSR despatched a number of Soviet and East European pilots to take the place of those who had left. On 28 September Premier Bulganin addressed a most polite but at the same time sobering letter to Premier Eden warning him against the dangers of his belligerent postures.[64]

Soviet Policy at the United Nations

The Anglo-French strategy during the diplomatic phase of the crisis for obtaining an imposed settlement having the sanctity of an international mandate did not succeed mainly because of active opposition of the Soviet Union and restraining influence of the United States. Nasser could not be forced to accept the 18-power proposals presented to him by Menzies. Nasser then brought an alternative proposal of his own for convening a conference of all the Canal users to deal with freedom of navigation, dues and maintenanee, that is, all matters save management and control, under an agreement which would give rights to all and be lodged with the United Nations, who would act as an arbiter. Britain and France could never agree to such a proposal as it would have been a negation of all their efforts at the first London Conference whose composition, timing and venue they had contrived in such a way as to obtain a majority decision in accordance with their premeditated plan. Now thanks to the astute American diplomacy the SCUA plan had proved nothing but a halting procedure.

By this time Britain and France had become disillusioned about the American role and disregarding the American wishes decided to take the issue to the United Nations, feeling that "if we successfully passed a mandatory resolution, Nasser would have to give way. If as was almost certain there was a Soviet veto, then force would be justified."[65] Their resort to the United Nations was described as a "procedure, not a policy".[66]

As on previous occasions, here again Washington was divided from Paris and London by differences of approach of a fundamental character. America refused to accept the Anglo-French thesis that the role of the United Nations was merely the "formal one" of approving the Anglo-French draft, that Egypt would naturally defy it and then there will be good reason to resort to direct action.[67]

The UN Security Council opened debate on 5 October on the Anglo-French complaint against Egypt's nationalization of the Suez Canal Company. It then adjourned to 8 October and went the following day into secret session to discuss the draft Anglo-French resolution, which asserted that 18-power proposals and the SCUA should bethe basis of negotiation.But the Soviets, backing Egypt's case, laid down three principles as a basis for such negotiations :

1. The establishment of a system of cooperation between Egypt and the Canal users with full recognition of sovereign rights of Egypt and the interests of the users.
2. The establishment of a system of tolls and charges which guaranteed users fair treatment and to exploitation, and
3. The setting aside of a reasonable portion of the Canal's revenues for improvements.[68]

On 8 October Egypt's representative Mahmoud Fawzi made his first principal speech in the Security Council. He was followed by Shepilov[69] who outrightly condemned the draft Anglo-American resolution, attacked the Suez Canal Company as thoroughly corrupt, imperialist, colonial system, "and charged that efforts to internationalize the Canal were the work of "reactionary elements" attempting to force Egypt to her knees and "serve a lesson to other people of the East."

The next important speech of Shepilov was delivered on 13 October during the continued discussion of the problem.[70] Before his speech Egyptian delegate Fawzi in his speech had accepted the "six principles" incorporated in the Anglo-French draft, which he had already approved during private negotiations with British and French representatives. However, he rejected the machinery proposed to implement them, but declared that Egypt was prepared for a settlement. Shepilov supported the Egyptian case almost word by word. He welcomed the "six principles" and praised the United Nations and Egyptian good will. He too denounced the operative parts of the Anglo-Freneh draft, which in no way stemmed from conversations which had taken place or from the work done at the Security Council. There were no legal or moral grounds why the Council should force on Egypt the institution of the self-executive advisory Committee. If this were done now, the negotiations in the future would be impossible. In this way Shepilov dismissed the SCUA. Only a few nations were going to claim particular functions in the Canal, functions that belonged to the Egyptian Authority. All this was not in the province of the Security Council, for the Canal was working well under Egyptian management. Since the United Nations had the dispute before it, a genuine safeguard existed for the fulfilment of Egypt's treaty obligations regarding the Canal. He, therefore, would not support the second part of the resolution. He asserted that the implementation part was tantamount to "coercion". When votes were taken that day the Soviet Union while approving the first part of the resolution containing the "six principles" vetoed the second part. Then the Seeurity Council adjourned without taking any further action.

London and Paris were badly defeated in their game. And as Eden remarked, "They had, in fact, worsened their position since their original intention of obtaining United Nations' approval for the proposed system of international operation of the Suez Canal was completely side-tracked.[71]

Cautious optimism prevailed at the conclusion of the Security Council deliberations, as Britain, France, and Egypt were expected to resume negotiations presided over by Secretary-General, Dag Hammarskjold. But the appearance was quite deceptive. Although negotiations continued throughout October, these contacts were maintained "more as a matter of form than with the earnest intention of reaching agreement."[72] The proceedings in the Security Council marked the end of one chapter and the opening of another.

About the outcome of the Security Council proceedings, Eden recalled, "These discussions bowed out the practical proposals of the eighteen powers, which were our minimum requirement for the security of the Canal. They were never allowed the limelight again. Though the Americans had been the first advocates of these proposals, the Administration showed no concern at their defeat by the Communist veto. . . I soon learnt that the Soviet Government regarded the proceedings at the United Nations as a victory for Egypt and for them. In this they were undoubtedly right."[73] Henceforth, the Anglo-French alliance detached itself from the United States and began coordinating its plans for the use of force.

Ever since mid-September the Soviet government had been seriously alarmed at the possibility of Western armed intervention in Egypt. In this connection, mention has already been made of the Soviet note of 15 September which described the Anglo-French military preparations as "dangerous provocations intended further to aggravate the situation.' And that the USSR would not stand aside because an "aggression in the area of the Near and Middle East touches on the security of the Soviet state." Similar sentiments were expressed throughout September and most of October. Premier Bulganin in his letters of 11, 28 September and 23 October to Eden and Mollet, which contain the finest example of reasonable pleading, civilized persuasion, moderation and restraint, delivered many a vague warnings.[74] The last one particularly came at a time when preparations were in hot progress for coordinated military action. In it supreme importance was attached to the United Nations and resolving the disputes through it. Satisfaction was expressed that the Security Council reached an "agreed decision" on principles furnishing a basis for an ultimate settlement of the Suez issue.

Throughout October Moscow expressed its apprehension of a concerted Western action. It did not believe in reports of rupture between the United States and her allies, instead it saw a basic unity of purpose between the three.

By this time the Israelis, in furthering their own national objectives, were in an advanced stage of planning a war against Egypt. Any sign of detente was to their disadvantage. When the Suez question was referred to the UN and Egypt committed herself to international negotiations, Israelis moved to sabotage the prospects of settlement by launching a full-fledged military attack on Jordan, even before the Council had started the debate. They again attacked the Jordanian police posts in the area of Qalqilya during the night of 10-11 October. This was strongly criticized by *Izvestia*.[75] By now Israel had entered into an agreement with France and Britain to make war. Qalqilya was a prelude to a full-scale invasion of the Sinai. The Suez conflict had been enmeshed with the Arab-Israeli conflict.

It is found that throughout the diplomatic phase of the crisis the Soviet Union, keeping in view its own national interests, played an active role by vigorously defending the sovereignty and territorial integrity of Egypt and enabling that country to maintain its independence and resist imperialist pressures at a critical juncture.[76]

Soviet Role During the Suez War

Military action against Egypt was first launched by Israel and then joined by Britain and France as planned beforehand.[77] Of the three parties, France and Israel had been collaborating against Nasser as early as 1954 when a Franco-Israeli arms deal was concluded. A second big arms deal was contracted next year in November which further modernized the Israeli army. The French were led to wish that they could save their Algerian colony only by liquidating Nasser with the help of the Israelis. Likewise, Britain also wanted to get rid of Nasser but all of them were restrained by the US. After a series of meetings between the leaders of the three countries they decided to act independently of the United States.[78] The final agreement was signed on 23 October at Sevres in a secret meeting. Israel invaded the Sinai in the night of 29-30 October. It was followed by the Anglo-French ultimatum and aerial attacks.

The Soviet representative at the United Nations, Arkady Sobolev, welcomed the American initiative in bringing the matter to the UN Security Council and demanded the Israeli aggression be immediately quashed. He also referred to the news just received that Britain and France had issued ultimatums to Egypt and Israel to keep ten miles away from the Suez Canal. It proves, the Soviet representative said, that Israel must have been encouraged to attack by those aggressive circles which were trying to find some pretext to move their troops into the region. He fully supported the American resolution condemning Israeli action and demanding withdrawal of the invading armies. The US resolution was vetoed by Britain and France. Thereupon the Soviet Union put a simple cease-fire resolution which too was vetoed. Meanwhile aerial bombing of Egypt had started.

On 31 October the Security Council resolved to convene a special emergency session of the Security Council to deal with the situation. The session opened on 1 November. The American draft resolution taking note of the Israeli invasion, Anglo-French military operations against Egypt, and interruption of traffic in the Suez Canal, called for immediate ceasefire. The resolution was supported by the USSR and passed the next day. Sobolev in his speech of 1 November referred to the conspiracy between the aggressors, urged for condemnation of aggression, immediate ceasefire and withdrawal, and appointment of a UN supervising commission.

The statement issued by the Soviet government on 31 October regarding the Israeli aggression said:

"Facts indicate that the obvious reason behind this Israeli invasion was to give the Western powers, primarily Britain and France, an excuse for bringing their troops into the territory of Arab states, particularly into the zone of the Suez Canal. The Western powers are screening their aggressive actions with references to the colonialist declaration made in 1950 by the USA, Britain and France, a declaration that was unanimously rejected by the Arab States . . .

"The Soviet government considers that the Security Council of the United Nations must for the sake of preserving peace and tranquillity in the Near and Middle East, take prompt measures towards ending the aggressive actions of Britain, France and Israel against Egypt, and towards the immediate withdrawal of the interventionist forces from Egyptian territory."[79]

The attack was conceived, a commentator charged, "with the object of crushing the national liberation movement of the Arab peoples" and "to restore the colonial system throughout the Middle East and North Africa."[80]

The Soviet statement of 31 October was very formal. Soviet passivity and indecision is also apparent from the move that the Soviet leaders proposed the next day. On 1 November it was announced in Moscow that President Voroshilov and Premier Bulganin had sent letters to President Sukarno of Indonesia and Prime Minister Nehru of India drawing their attention to the desirability of calling an emergency session of the Bandung conference to urge the interventionist parties to stop their action and withdraw their forces forthwith.[81]

But Soviet reaction, hitherto in a low-key, intensified on 4 November when Moscow sent a note[82] to the governments of Britain and France, which taking note of the gravity of tripartite aggression and reminding of speeches of the Soviet representative at the United Nations, expressed concern over closing of certain zones of eastern Mediterranean and northern Red Sea to merchant shipping. This virtually blockaded the Suez Canal which was impermissible under the 1888 Convention. "The Government of the Soviet Union", the note stated, "resolutely protests against these unlawful actions taken by the United Kingdom and France and declares that responsibility for all possible consequences of such actions rests with the British and French government."

Now tangible Soviet intervention came only on 5 November when the Soviet government delivered the famous messages to the heads of state of the USA, UK, France and Israel as well as to the President of UN Security Council.[83] At dawn that day the Anglo-French paratroopers landed at Port Said.

In Shepilov's message to the UN Security Council and Bulganin's letter to the American President it was suggested that Britain and France be requested to order a ceasefire within the next twelve hours, and that if they refused, a joint Soviet-American force be despatched to halt the aggression. The Soviets threatened Britain, France and Israel with terrible reprisals, hinting at the use of nuclear weapons, if they did not desist.

There is no doubt that during the period between 29 October and 5 November, that is, in the period of the eight days embracing the Israeli invasion and occupation of the Sinai, the Anglo-French ultimatums of 30 October, bombardment of the Egyptian territory, UN call on 2 November for a ceasefire, and the actual landing of the Anglo-French forces in Egypt, the Soviets were unwilling to intervene effectively in defence of Egypt. There appear to be two reasons for Soviet indecision and inaction: Revolt in Hungary and apprehension of a possible American intervention in the crisis. The numerous instances of fundamental difference between America and her allies, the utterances of Eisenhower and Dulles to the effect that they were against the use of force, did not convince the Soviet Union of the neutrality of the USA in the crisis. It was not until the US had openly censured her allies that the Soviets were assured of America's revulsion from its allies' actions and its concern to stop them.

Having crushed the revolt in Hungary and having assured themselves of America's neutrality and even hostility towards its allies, the USSR turned to intervene on behalf of Egypt at the minimum of cost. Soviet intervention when it came took two distinct forms: firstly, it assumed a threatening posture (i.e., veiled threats of using nuclear missiles against the aggressors contained in Soviet Notes sent to Britain, France and

Israel on 5 November; and the threat of sending Soviet volunteers to fight with the Egyptians as announced on 6 and 10 November. Secondly, it adopted the course of cooperation with the United States. The Soviet Union while issuing threats to America's allies, had at the same time, appealed to the President of the USA for cooperation and sending of joint forces to the area to halt aggression. The next day again, the Soviet representative at the United Nations repeated the Soviet request for joint intervention to halt the aggression.

This conciliatory and cooperative gesture in conjunction with the previous indifference of the Soviet Union between 29 October and 4 November has been marshalled as an evidence in support of the view that the Soviet threats had no substance, no effect and were a mere bluff, although it seems Soviet moves at the time were taken seriously.[84] Sir William Hayter, Britain's Ambassador in Moscow at the time of the Suez crisis says: "Its intention was not to persuade the (British) Prime Minister but to put pressure on him, or at least to appear to be doing so. I have never known for certain how great a part it played in the decision to call off the Suez operation, which was in fact taken the following morning. Personally I later came to believe that this decision was taken on other grounds, and moreover that the Russians when they sent their letter knew our collapse was inevitable and imminent and cashed in on this by delivering threats they were sure they would never have to carry out, thus enabling themselves to pose as saviours of the Arabs."[85] He further observes that the Soviet government had threatened Britain and France and destroyed their own policy of detente with the West in order to "maintain their prestige with the Arabs."[86] Similarly, John Erickson is of the opinion that these threats were not genuine as they evaporated the moment the Americans threatened with counter measures. The threat to send volunteers "was made in such a way as to be known to potential volunteers until the war was over. Russian policy during the critical three months was to avoid getting left out of any settlement. During the super-critical week, which coincided with the Hungarian revolution, the Russians improvised, took their bombers away from Egypt and issued threats which were without credibility or effect in the West."[87]

In between most Western estimates of the Soviet moves as an outright bluff and Soviet extravagant claims that it was only the Soviet threat and not the moral and political pressure of the USA that had saved the Arabs from the "predatory imperialism" a relatively moderate estimate of the Soviet interventionist behaviour is that Soviet threats constituted one factor among many that contributed to the eventual defeat of aggression. The threats had a direct bearing on the American attitude the next day. Anxious to halt further Soviet moves the United States put the maximum pressure on its allies to retreat. According to one French account, the American Ambassador in Paris, A.C. Douglous Dillon, called on Prime Minister Mollet at midnight with a message saying that "if you continue with your culpable attitude do not count on us."[88] According to Dillon himself, the Soviet threats were "the only new element that had come in." He did not think that Britain and France stopped because of moral suasion.[89] Susan strong holds that, reminiscent as the Soviet threat to send volunteers was of the Chinese government warning to send "volunteers" to North Korea, "the threat was undoubtedly felt to be more menacing than it appeared on the surface."[90] According to Robertson, "By threatening two major powers with rocket war, the Soviet Union had taken what constituted the gravest and most aggressive diplomatic action in its history. Propaganda, obviously one motive, was too glib to be the only one."[91]

We may safely conclude that the intention of the Soviet Union was never to fight for Egypt as it would have entailed the risk of direct confrontation with the USA. It is well known that when the combined invasion took place, the Soviet personnel and the bombers stationed in Egypt were ordered out for shelter in the neighbouring countries in order to avoid giving any proof of military association with Egyptian resistance for the fear that the United States might ultimately join its allies in the war.[92]

Soviet policy throughout the crisis was cautions, rather than reckless, deliberate rather than impetuous and conservative, rather than radical. Soviet threats represented more than extraordinary diplomatic pressure in favour of Egypt. They were motivated probably by an awareness of what the Soviet Union stood to lose as a result of the Western or UN action. They were meant to extract the maximum political capital for the Soviet Union at the minimum of cost.

The Soviet attitude towards the formation of a United Nations Emergency Force for the area betrayed a basic concern with the narrow self-interest. To understand the Soviet opposition to the Canadian plan one should look back at the General Assembly proceedings since 3 November. In Assembly's meeting of 3 November the Soviet block together with the Afro-Asian and Arab delegations had demanded immediate withdrawal and sanctions against the aggressors. But the United States now assumed a pro-allies posture. Its delegate Cabot Lodge submitted two draft resolutions, one for a five-member committee to take the place of the old Palestine Conciliation Commission and another for clearance of the Suez Canal in implementation of the "six principles". The Lodge plan was opposed by the Soviets on the grounds that it smothered the main issue, the halting of aggression. At this stage India put a draft for an immediate ceasefire and Canada produced the plan for setting up a UN emergency force.[93] By 7 November the Soviet representative had come out firmly against the UNEF plan.[94] He resented the fact that this force had become a "condition" which the Western powers and Israel were using to delay their evacuation of Egypt. He saw in its creation an attempt to bring about a settlement of the Suez question favourable to the UK and France. The occupation of the Suez Canal Zone by an international force meant removing the Canal from the Egyptian hands. The Soviets were afraid that the force once established on Egyptian soil will be to the advantage of the West. Secondly, it created a dangerous precedent for UN intervention in similar possible situations within the Soviet bloc.

On 15 November Premier Bulganin sent a letter to Premier Eden stating that in view of the continued presence of aggressor troops on Egyptian soil "there is no need for such an international force. However, taking into account the fact that the government of Egypt has in principle given its consent to this, the Soviet government has no objection to the introduction of the UN force, having in view that it can be located on both sides of the demarcation line between Israel and Egypt, established by the armistice agreement. Those troops should not be located in the Suez Canal Zone...."[95]

Then on 23 November speaking at a plenary meeting of the General Assembly, Shepilov took note of the continued presence of invading troops in Egypt. Referring to the function of the UN troops in Egypt, their location and length of stay, he declared that the Soviet government fully supported the Egyptian position. When the British and French troops left Port Said, the UN troops could have no function either in Port Said or the Canal Zone.[96]

The Arab-Israeli Conflict, 1957—67

Prior to the Suez War, the Soviets had supported the Arabs because of their anti-Westernism. They gave them arms against the West. They opposed the pro-Western line of Israeli government but never questioned the fact of Israel's statehood. At this stage Soviet interest was limited to participation in any deliberations over or settlement in the region. This became clear from Soviet statement of 9 February 1956[97] and the statement of 13 February.[98] The same point was stressed in the Soviet Foreign Ministry's statement of 17 April[99] in which the Soviets declared that (i) they were ready to render the necessary support to measures of the UN aimed at exploring ways and means for strengthening peace in the Palestine area ; (ii) that in their view measures must be taken in the immediate future to ease the existing tension without interference from outside ; and (iii) that if peace were to be maintained the matter must be handled in such a way as to lead to a lasting settlement on a mutually acceptable basis, taking due account of the just national interests of the parties to abstain from any action which might aggravate the situation on the Armistice Lines. The Soviets expressed their readiness to facilitate, together with other states, a peaceful settlement of the outstanding questions. This statement completely ignored the prevailing Arab position on the preconditions of a peace settlement. According to Eytan,[100] the statement aroused hopes in Israel as it came nearer to Israeli position of arriving at a settlement by direct negotiations and agreement. The Arabs understood the Soviet declaration in the same sense and immediately criticized it on this account.

The statement issued in London on 26 April 1956, after conclusion of talks between Premier Bulganin and USSR Supreme Soviet Presidium member Khrushchev and British Premier Eden went in the same direction. The Soviets were in complete accord with the Western position on the West Asian region.[101]

However, as Soviet influence increased in the area in the aftermath of the Suez War, the Soviet Union abandoned this line. During the decade 1957-1967 its policy definitely relied on Arab-Israeli polarization and intensification of regional tensions as means of further consolidating Soviet influence. This line was pursued despite persisting Soviet-Arab political differences on such questions as the nature and purpose of Arab nationalism, Arab unity, Arab socialism and role of the local communist parties.

After the turbulent events of 1958, the region seemed to relapse into an atmosphere of relative calm throughout the next two years. Taiwan and Berlin crises[102] eclipsed this area. Soviet bloc military and diplomatic support to the Arab countries continued unabated. Soviet media continued to depict Israel as a tool of Western imperialism.[103] Reacting to stepping up of the American arms supplies to Israel one Soviet commentator saw it as part of a world-wide arms build up. Israel was being armed with missiles and conventional arms to enable her to realize her aggressive plans of expansion.[104] During 1963 Soviet diplomatic relations with Israel were strained as Moscow sent a censorious note to Tel Aviv over its armament drive.

Khrushchev's visit to Egypt in May 1964 to inauguarate the opening part of the Aswan Dam was the high-water mark of Soviet support to the Arabs during this period. However, speaking before the Egyptian National Assembly he supported the just demands of the Arab states but stuck to the basic Soviet stand that force should not be used to settle border disputes. In 1958 some Rumanian Jews were allowed to migrate to Israel but during 1965, according to Abba Eban, some two thousand Jews reached Israel from the USSR.[105] But the winds of ehange came with Premier Kosygin's visit to Cairo from 10 to 18 May which was linked to a shift in Soviet policy towards the eastern Mediterranean and the Arab East.

REFERENCES

1. Cf. Guy Wint and Peter Calvocoressi, *The Middle East Crisis* (London, 1957).
2. For a survey of Arab-Western relations see John Marlowe, *Arab Nationalism and British Imperialism* (London, 1961) ; Eiizabeth Monroe, *Britain's Moment in the Middle East* (London, 1963) ; Erskine Childers. *The Road to Suez.* A Study of Western-Arab Relations (London, 1966).
3. *Survey of International Affairs, 1951* (London, 1954), pp. 258.
4. *Survey of International Affairs, 1955* (London, 1957), p. 116.
5. *Survey of International Affairs, 1954* (London, 1957), pp. 202-213; *Survey of International Affairs, 1955-56* (London, 1960), pp. 24-32.
6. Patrick Seale, *The Struggle for Syria* (London, 1965), pp. 186-212.
7. Wint and Calvocoressi (note 1), pp. 48-54.
8. Fayez A. Sayegh, *The Dynamics of Neutralism in the Arab World* (Chicago, 1964); Leonard Binder, "Nasserism : the Protest Movement in the Middle East", in Binder, ed., *The Ideological Revolution in the Middle East* (New York, 1964), pp. 209-211.
9. For texts of the Soviet statements see *Documents on International Affairs, 1955* (London, 1959), pp. 300-304; *Documents on International Affairs, 1956* (London, 1960). pp. 59-61.
10. *The Times*, 12 September 1955.
11. *New York Times*, 27 September 1955.
12. Pierre Rondot, *The Changing Patterns of the Middle East* (New York, 1962), p. 149.
13. Uri Ra'anan, *The USSR Arms the Third World* (Michigan, 1969).
14. Walter Z. Laqueur, *The Soviet Union and the Middle East*, (London, 1959), pp, 218-19.
15. R'anan (*note* 13), p. 20.
16. Dwight D. Eisenhower, *The White House Years.* Waging Peace, 1956-1961 (London, 1966) (London, 1966), pp. 24-25.
17. Tom Little, *Modern Egypt* (London, 1969), pp. 160 ff.
18. Sherman Adams, *First Hand Report,* The Story of the Eisenhower Administration (New York, 1961), p. 249.

19. *Arab Scribe*, April 1964, p. 83.
20. *Ibid.*, p. 84.
21. Text in the *Times*, 12 September 1956; also in D.C. Watt, ed., *Documents on the Suez Crisis* (London, 1957).
22. Hugh Thomas, *The Suez Affair* (London, 1967), pp. 39-40.
23. Anthony Nutting, *No End of A Lesson*. The story of Suez (London, 1967), p. 45.
24. *The Times* 1 August 1956.
25. Sir Anthony Eden, *Memoirs*: *Full Circle* (London, 1960), 4. 426.
26. *Ibid.*, p. 434.
27. Childers (*note* 2), p. 185.
28. Seale (note 6), pp. 250 ff.
29. Anthony Moncrief and Peter Calvocoressi, eds., *Suez—Ten Years After* (London, 1967), p. 36.
30. Cf. *Survey of International Affairs, 1956-58* (London, 1962), pp. 53-54.
31. Terrence Robertson, *Crisis*—The Inside Story of the Suez Conspiracy (London, 1965), p. xvi.
32. Childers (note 2), p. 175.
33. *Ibid.*, p. 179.
34. Charles D. Cremeans, *The Arabs and the World* (New York, 1963), p. 151.
35. Eisenhower (*note* 16), pp. 43-44.
36. Herman Finer, *Dulles Over Suez* (London, 1964), p. 62.
37. *Ibid.*
38. Eden (*note* 25), p. 437.
39. Watt, ed. (*note* 21), p. 6.
40. Laqueur (*note* 14), pp, 232-233.
41. *Current Digest of the Soviet Press* 8(32), 12 September 1956.
42. The text in *New Times* (19) May 1956.
43. D.F. Fleming, *The Cold War and Its Origin* (London, 1958), 823 ; Andre Fontaine, *History of the Cold War* (London, 1970), p. 171.
44. Eden (*note* 25), pp. 448-49.
45. *Facts-on-File* 22-28 August 1956.
46. *Ibid.*
47. *Soviet News*, 10 August 1956.
48. *Ibid.*, 16 August 1956.
49. *Ibid.*, 17 August 1956.
50. Eisenhower (*note* 16), p. 45.

51. Eden (*note* 25), p. 443.
52. *Soviet News*, 24 August 1956.
53. *Ibid.*, 27 August 1956.
54. *The Times*, 28 August 1956.
55. Text in Thomas (*note* 22), p. 186.
56. Finer (*note* 36), p. 215.
57. *Survey of International Affairs, 1956-58*, pp. 34-38.
58. *Documents of International Affairs, 1956*, pp. 334-38.
59. Thomas (*note* 22), p. 83.
60. Eden (*note* 25), p. 492.
61. *Documents of International Affairs*, 1956, pp. 248 ff.
62. *Ibid.*, pp. 223-30.
63. *CDSP* 8 (38), 31 October, 1956.
64. Text in Thomas (*note* 22), pp. 94 ff.
65. Thomas (*note* 22), p. 72.
66. *Survey of International Affairs, 1956-58*, p. 43.
67. *Ibid.*
68. Watt, ed. (*note* 21), p. 18.
69. Text of Shepilov's speech in *Soviet News*, 9-10 October 1956.
70. Text in *Soviet News*, 15 October 1956.
71. Eden (*note* 25), p. 505.
72. *Survey of International Affairs, 1956-58*, p. 47.
73. Eden (*note* 25), p. 509.
74. Texts in Thomas (*note* 22), pp. 180-95.
75. *CDSP* 8(41), 21 November 1956.
76. For a contrary opinion see Oles M. Smolansky, "Moscow and the Suez Crisis, 1956: A Reapraisal". *Political Science Quarterly* 80(6), December 1965, pp. 581-605.
77. Thomas (*note* 22), pp. 85-120; Moncrief (*note* 29), pp. 59-74.
78. *Survey of International Affairs 1956-58*, pp. 49-50.
79. *Documents on International Affairs 1956*, pp. 269 ff.
80. Y. Bochkaryov's commentary, *New Times*, 22 November 1956.
81. Text in *Soviet News*, 2 November 1956.
82. *Documents on International Affairs, 1956*, pp. 280-81.
83. Texts in *Documents on International Affairs 1956*, pp. 286-94.
84. Eden (*note* 25), pp. 654-55.
85. Sir William Hayter, *The Kremlin and the Embassy* (London, 1966), p. 146.

86. *Ibid.*, p. 154.
87. *Listener*, 21 July 1966, p. 78.
88. Thomas (*note* 22), pp. 142-43.
89. Emile Lengyel, *Egypt's Role in World Affairs* (New York, 1957), p. 82.
90. Susan Strang, "Suez and After",in the *Year Book of World Affairs*, 1957, pp. 76-103.
91. Robertson (*note* 31), 256-57.
92. Moncrief (*note* 29), pp. 49-50.
93. Finer (*note* 36). p. 403.
94. *GAOR* 1956, 562nd Mtg., pp. 71, 89.
95. *Documents on International Affairs, 1956*, pp. 320-23.
96. *Soviet News*, 29 November 1956.
97. *Survey of International Affairs, 1955-56*, p. 276.
98. *Soviet News*, 18 April 1956.
99. *Ibid.*
100. *Walter, Eytan The First Ten Years* : A Diplomatic History of Israel (New York, 1958), p. 143.
101. *New Times*, (19) May 1956.
102. *Survey of International Affairs, 1959-60* (Oxford 1964), pp. 333-381.
103. E.G., Radio Moscow's commentary in Arabic, 13 December 1960, *SWB*/IV, 2 January 1961.
104. *Izvestia*, 3 October 1962.
105. Abba Eban, *Voice of Israel* (New York, 1968), p. 167.

CHAPTER IV

The War of 1967 and Reappraisal

The Crisis of May 1967

The Soviet Factor was not the only factor, but one of the many that precipitated the crisis of May and War of June 1967. Nor was the crisis a result solely of the Arab-Israeli conflict. The war would probably not have broken if the two were left alone. What happened before the Suez Crisis of 1956 is most pertinent, even indispensable, for an understanding of the events leading to the war of 1967. The Arab world was torn apart as before by rival regimes, contrasting ideologies, competitive bids for leadership and diverse orientations of domestic and foreign policy. If on the one hand, the Yemeni Civil War (started 1961) and the Egyptian intervention in it had intensified the antagonism between the "progressive" states led by Egypt and the "reactionary" regimes led by the Saudi Kingdom, on the other hand the breakup of the union between Egypt and Syria in 1961 had turned Damascus and

Cairo into two rival centres of the ideology of Arab renaissance. In the Arab Cold War the chief weapon with the contestants was anti-Israel propaganda and mutual recrimination.

Syria was the centre of events which led in quick succession to the crisis of May 1967. The government formed in February 1965 by the pro-Soviet left wing of the Ba'ath Party after toppling the government of the moderates attracted the special attention of the Soviet leaders as it was for the first time in Arab history that two communists were included in the Syrian cabinet. During 1966 and early 1967 Syria had repeated armed clashes with Israel in the wake of Israel's illegal occupation of the demilitarized zone established under the Armistice Agreement of 1949. The Soviet were quite alarmed when Israeli reprisals threatened the survival of the new regime already troubled by domestic resistance. They were fascinated by the new regime as it provided a justification for Soviet forward policy in the Arab East and held out a promise of collaboration in effecting the Soviet strategy in the eastern Mediterranean which was then taking shape. Hence in late 1966 and early 1967 preservation of the tottering Syrian regime assumed highest priority in Soviet thinking.[1] To bolster the Syrian position and deter Israel, the Soviet leaders persuaded Egypt in November 1966 to conclude a mutual defence pact with Syria. Declarations by Israeli leaders that the Israeli forces will march into Damascus alarmed the Soviets who launched a massive propaganda campaign against Israeli troop concentration on Syrian borders and an impending attack. Finally, the massive Israeli raid into Syria by Israel on 7 April 1967 acted like a danger signal for them.[2] The Syrian-Egyptian mutual defence pact of 1966 had proved ineffective in deterring Israel. The Soviets, therefore, sought to compromise Egypt into a closer identification of its armed forces for any future eventuality. On 13 May they informed Egypt of massive Israeli troop concentration on Syrian borders for an attack on 17 May. Nasser ordered the mobilization of the Egyptian armed forces on 14 May. Although Soviet warnings about Israeli intentions regarding Syria were mainly responsible for Egypt's decision to mobilize, there is no evidence which could suggest that beyond seeking a limited defensive objective the Soviets went to incite the

Egyptians to initiate the series of actions and events starting with the demand of evacuation of the United Nations Emergency Force from the Sinai on 16 May (it withdrew on 18 May and ending with the announcement of the blockade of Aqaba on 23 May.[3]

In examining Soviet responsibility for and Soviet role during the June 1967 War two questions are most important : (i) who incited the Egyptians to demand the withdrawal of the UNEF from the Sinai and reimpose the blockade of Aqaba ? and (ii) who prevented Egypt when it was fully prepared to go to war, from launching the attack so that Israelis were able to launch a surprise attack and defeat the Egyptian army within six days ? There is firm evidence to show that the first two measures were the responsibility of the Egyptian leadership itself which seemed to act on national and regional considerations. The large responsibility for the second outcome falls on the Soviet Union which tied the hands of President Nasser probably at the behest of America without getting a similar guarantee of restraint on Israel. The answers to these two questions have afforded two contending explanations of the Soviet role in precipitating the May 1967 crisis and inaction during the June War. One is that the Soviet Union intended all that happened—the war, Arab defeat and their increased dependence on the Soviets. Whetten, for instance, holds that between 1966 and 1967 Moscow "adopted a new approach, hoping that deliberate escalation in Arab-Israeli tensions would proportionally increase the Arabs' psychological, military and political dependence on Moscow. The Soviet reports of Israeli troop deployments along the Syrian border in April 1967 were a deliberate incremental use of tension to promote these aims."[4] A second explanation is that the Soviet Union had a limited objective of deterring Israeli invasion of Syria and it assumed that if tension rose the UN Secretary General U Thant would follow the procedure adopted by the late Dag Hammarskjold and defuse the situation. The Soviet leaders were taken by surprise when Nasser demanded the evacuation of the UNEF from the Sinai and when he reimposed the blockade of Aqaba. But since these moves had already been taken the Soviets had no option but to support the Arab position in the Security Council. Probably they thought that if anything can go wrong, it will. The Soviet statement of 24 May clearly implied that their support to the Arabs was subject to their undertaking not to initiate hostilities in a region so close to the Soviet borders. After the reimposition of the blockade, Kosygin is reported to have told the visiting Egyptian War Minister Shams-el-Din Badran : "You have won a political victory. So it is time now to compromise, to work politically."[5] Stephens has cited French diplomatic sources for the information that the Soviet leaders told Egyptian and Syrian ambassadors in Moscow that the USSR "would not support them if they attacked Israel, and that the Soviet Union will not back them militarily if they were attacked by Israel alone."[6] Acting on Israeli intelligence reports about an impending Egyptian attack on Israel, Washington probably pressed Moscow to restrain Egypt. Thereupon, the Soviet Ambassador in Cairo V.A. Vinogradov is said to have wakened Nasser in the night of 27 May to warn him against firing the first shot. Perhaps the Soviet leaders overlooked the need of seeking a similar restraint on Israel.[7] However, President L.B. Johnson claims that he persuaded the Israeli Foreign Minister Abba Eban when he visited Washington on 26 May that "the USA was committed to ensure Israeli passage through Aqaba and to try first the diplomatic means." On his assurance the Israeli Cabinet on 28 May decided to postpone military action. But when no breakthrough came through the United Nations, the Israelis by 3 June decided to move on their own. Israeli motivations may have been the growing threat of a combined Arab military action, the economic strains of Israeli mobilization and the futility of the diplomatic means.[8]

Laqueur seems to subscribe to the second interpretation of the Soviet motives : "For Syria's actions and Nasser's initial decisions the Soviet Union bears a large part of the responsibility. But its intention was not, as many believed during the early days of the crisis, to create a 'second front' in the Middle East. It was, in all probability, more modest in its predicament. Neither Washington nor Moscow thought the conflict would lead to war."[9] Lall, at that time India's representative at the United Nations, has testified that "...the UAR did not consult with the Soviet Union about the withdrawal of the UNEF. Moscow was taken by surprise by Cairo's demand for withdrawal and Soviet diplomats assiduously inquired from all who might have some special knowledge of Arab intentions why Nasser had taken this step and how far he was prepared to go. Similarly, the action of the UAR in regard to the Gulf of Aqaba, which Nasser recognized would take the Middle East to the brink of war, was taken without prior information to the Soviet Union. Though the Soviet Union was confronted with these unexpected events, its position in the Middle East remained one of yielding to none in the level of support that it would give to its allies and friends."[10] Equally plausible is Glassman's explanation of the ambivalent, hesitant nature of Soviet policy during this period. The key elements, according to her that determined the evolution of events before and during the war were: (i) the desire of the Soviet Union to support the "progressive" Arab states in its search for influence and yet, at the same time, this desire was tempered by the desire to avoid direct confrontation with the West in regional conflicts; (ii) the thaw in its relations with the United States may or may not have been a determining factor but strategic balance probably played an important role in Moscow's decision to avoid confrontation with the US (the Soviets were yet to achieve strategic parity with the US and strategic mobility); and (iii) the Soviets were not confident that they could contain any conflict in which they were involved to the local level.[11] According to Draper, "The Soviet Union never took a position on the Egyptian right to close the Straits of Tiran to Iarael. The reason for this unusual diffidence was probably the potential effect of the Egyptian claim on the Soviets' own maritime interests. The entrance to the Black Sea through the Dardanelles and the Bosporus is at least as much in Turkish waters as the Strait of Tiran is in Egyptian territorial waters. For this, if for no other reason, the Soviets preferred to base themselves on alleged Israeli plans to invade Syria rather than on the merits of the Egyptian case dealing with the Straits of

Tiran, which was after all, the immediate *cousus belli* of the third Arab-Israeli war."[12]

When the matter was finally brought before the emergency session of the UN Security Council on 24-30 May, Soviet delegate Nikolai Fedorenko voiced strong backing for the Arab cause in the present crisis and repeated the arguments raised in a Soviet government statement on 23 May in which Moscow blamed Israel for fomenting the trouble. In the end, Fedorenko asserted "The Soviet delegation would like to confirm once again that we did not and do not see sufficient grounds for any consultation, let alone urgent consultations, special consultations, and so on. All this further supercharges the atmosphere."[13] At the reconvened Security Council meeting on 29 May, he tried to sidetrack the blockade issue by insisting that "if the Security Council is now to consider in all seriousness the situation which is developing in the Near East, the situation must be considered in connection with the well-founded complaint submitted to the Council by the United Arab Republic."[14] Till the outbreak of the war on 5 June Soviet commentators continued to accuse the USA of hypocrisy and inciting Israel to provoke a conflict in order to strengthen its imperialist positions and protect its oil interests in the region and to distract attention from the position of 'deadlock' in Vietnam.[15]

Soviet acquiescence in and support of the Arab position was responsible for Egyptian self-complacency. On 29 May Nasser reported to the Egyptian National Assembly that after his meeting with Soviet Premier Kosygin in Moscow on 26-28 May, the UAR War Minister Shams Badran "relayed to me a message from Premier Kosygin saying that the Soviet Union stands with us in this battle and will not allow any country to interfere, so that the state of affairs prevailing before 1956 may be restored."[16]

In retrospect, the War of 1967 appears to be a child of Soviet miscalculations and Arab muddleheadedness and self-complacency. The Soviet government was excessively obsessed with the Israeli threat to the leftist regime in Syria. They had blown the threat out of all proportions thus prodding Nasser to go to the brink in order to halt a possible Israeli march into Damascus. But once Nasser mobilized his armed forces he expanded his aim to the restoration of the status quo of 1956. He could not retreat and he could not go to war in face of the great-power pressure.

Did the Soviets warn Egypt of the outbreak of hostilities? Evidently, the Egyptian high-command had put the armed forces on the alert. There appeared to be enough warning, indeed. Thus, Soviet embarrassment over the summary liquidation of the Egyptian and other air forces and collapse of the armies posed more a problem of prestige for them than mere loss of arms and equipment. Domestic weaknesses were soon diagnosed as the principal cause of demoralization. When the Soviets decided to rehabilitate the Arab armies they did so on condition that necessary administrative and social reforms were instituted and military training was imparted under close Soviet supervision and guidance.[17]

Soviet Role During and After the June War

The War of June 1967 ended in a quick collapse of the Arab armies equipped with Soviet weapons over a decade. Faced with the war, the Soviet Union had three alternatives: either to intervene, or keep passive or stop the war. It ignored the Arab charges of American collusion with Israel and their call for Soviet military intervention. It chose the course of seeking an early end of the war in cooperation with the USA. Soon after the outbreak of hostilities on 5 June, Soviet Premier Kosygin is reported to have activated the Moscow-Washington "hotline" for the first time since August 1963, to inform President Johnson that the Soviets had no intention of intervening in the war unless the US stepped in, called upon the United States to restrain Israel and expressed Moscow's desire to seek an early ceasefire through the United Nations.[18] Washington on its part assured of its intention to use all its influence to bring the hostilities to an end.

Assured of American non-intervention, the Soviet Union proceeded to stop the war. A Soviet Government statement on 5 June declared support for the Arab states, called on Israel to stop its aggression immediately and unconditionally and withdraw its forces behind the armistice lines. It also called upon other states to do all in their power to restore peace and on the United Nations to condemn Israel and take prompt steps to restore peace. At the UN Security Council the Soviet Union introduced a draft resolution condemning Israel for its aggression, demanding immediate ceasefire and withdrawal of its forces behind the 4 June borders.

However, on the first day of war the Egyptians were slow to realize the magnitude of their defeat and lost their chance of an immediate settlement and mutual withdrawal from the Sinai. President Johnson has recalled : "At the suggestion of Soviet UN Ambassador Nikolai Fedorenko, Goldberg met with the UAR representative, El Kony. He urged the Egyptians to move quickly. He stressed that this might be the last chance for a quick settlement and mutual withdrawal from the Sinai. But Cairo was not prepared to make commitments on June 5. The Arabs hoped to obtain a ceasefire and withdrawal of Israeli forces only. *They pushed Moscow hard to work for that and that alone.* So there was no action in the United Nations on the first day of war. But there was plenty of action in the war zone. Israeli forces pushed forward hour by hour."[19] (emphasis added).

By the evening of 6 June when the extent of their defeat became known to the Arabs themselves, Moscow dropped its insistence on the withdrawal clause and supported an American-sponsored draft which merely called for an immediate ceasefire. When Israel ignored the ceasefire demand by the superpowers and began its drive towards Damascus, the USSR on 7 June sponsored another UN demand for a ceasefire and sent a note[20] to Israel warning that if the ceasefire were not observed diplomatic relations would be broken and the USSR would "implement other necessary measures". On 9 June Moscow convened a hasty summit conference of the Warsaw Pact member-states which issued a communique[21] threatening decisive action if Israel did not immediately accept the proposed ceasefire. On 10 June, the last day of the war, Premier Kosygin used the "hotline" again and "accused Israel of ignoring all Security Council resolutions for a ceasefire. Kosygin said a 'very crucial moment' had now arrived. He spoke of the possibility of 'independent decision' by Moscow. He foresaw the risk of a 'grave catastrophe' and stated that unless Israel unconditionally halted operations within the next few hours, the Soviet Union would take "necessary actions, including military".[22] (President Johnson responded by ordering the Sixth Fleet to be 50 miles off the Syrian coast to intervene if necessary on Israel's behalf.) His account opens the speculation that a looming superpower confrontation was instrumental in bringing the fighting to an abrupt end and acceptance by Israel and Syria of the UN-sponsored ceasefire.[23] Soviet intervention at this point, when Israeli army was poised for a march into Damascus, signified the vital stake the USSR had developed in the survival of the "progressive" regimes. In the words of Whetten, "The first indications of the nature and scope of Soviet interest in the crisis were revealed even during the war, namely, that the vital centres and existing regimes of its sponsored States must remain immune from Israeli attack. This remained the fundamental Soviet position till 1973."[24] The USSR and East European states severed diplomatic relations with Israel on 10 June. The Soviet decision communicated in a note given to the Israeli Ambassador to the USSR also warned that "unless Israel halted immediately its military actions" against Syria, the Soviet Union "jointly with other peaceloving states, will undertake sanctions against Israel, with all the consequences flowing therefrom."[25]

At the UN Security Council on 14 June a Soviet draft resolution calling for condemnation of Israel and the immediate withdrawal of its forces behind the 1949 armistice lines was defeated. As a result of this failure, the Soviet Union placed the request on 13 June for the convening of an emergency special session of the UN General Assembly, which eventually started on 19 June to consider the problems created by the Arab-Israeli war. Meanwhile, the Central Committee of the Communist Party of the Soviet Union in a resolution on 21 June reaffirmed its support to the Arabs and promised all necessary diplomatic and military assistance to liquidate the consequences of Israeli aggression.[26] While Premier Kosygin led the Soviet delegation to attend the emergency session of the General Assembly, President Nikolai Podgorny led a goodwill mission to Egypt on 21-23 June and to Syria and Iran on 1-4 July to discuss further Soviet aid to the Arab States.

Mr Kosygin inaugurated the emergency special session of the General Assembly by recounting Israel's actions throughout the crisis and strongly condemned its aggression against the Arab states.[27] A draft resolution moved by him was to "vigorously condemn Israel's aggressive activities and the continuing occupations by Israel of part of the territory of the UAR, Syria and Jordan, which constitutes an act of recognized aggression", and "demanded that Israel should immediately and unconditionally withdraw all its forces from the territory of those states to positions behind the armistice lines."[28] The USA on 20 June introduced a counter-draft (not put to vote) calling for scrupulous observance of the ceasefire with a view to establishing stable and durable peace in the region achieved through negotiated arrangements and based on mutual recognition of political independence and territorial integrity of the states concerned, freedom of navigation in international waters, a just and equitable solution to the refugee problem and recognition of the right of all sovereign nations to exist in peace and security. A third draft was tabled by the Latin American states. Apparently anxious to come with some measure of achievement from the emergency session Soviet Foreign Minister Mr Gromyko was reported to have worked out behind the scene a compromise draft with the US delegate tying the withdrawal of Israeli forces to a termination of belligerency in the area. In view of the violent Arab reaction to this proposition, the Soviets did not sponsor this plan (ironically the same position was later embodied in Resolution 242).[29] The Soviet delegation then supported the non-aligned draft. To assuage Arab feelings, Soviet commentators tried hard to convince the Arabs that the Soviet Union was not working with the USA to evolve principles of a West Asian settlement.[30] When votes were taken on 4 July, none of the drafts could obtain a two-thirds majority due to behind-the-scene American pressures. On 5 July the meeting was adjourned to 12 July. Eventually the General Assembly on 21 July voted to adjourn *sine die* returning the discussion of the crisis meanwhile to the security Council. During the special session Premier Kosygin met President Johnson for an exchange of personal views on major problems of the world in two separate sessions on 23 and 25 June at Glassboro, New Jersey. Although fundamental differences persisted, the two sides expressed their agreement to disagree.[31]

Security Council Resolution 242

When the Security Council met again to take up the problem on 9-22 November, it was to discuss an American draft tabled on 9 November and a Soviet draft submitted on 20 November.[32] The gaps between the two positions were eventually filled by a compromise draft presented by the British delegate Lord Caradon, which seemingly bridged the unbridgeable positions of the belligerents and their respective superpower patrons. It laid down the principles of a peaceful settlement in the area. After haggling with the American delegate for a more definite use of terms, the Soviet delegate eventually acquiesced in the ambiguous and loose constructions as devised by the sponsor. This was passed as Resolution 242 on 22 November. This and other such UN declarations were mostly *pro forma*. Their loose construction and vague phrasing lent them to divergent interpretations by the local parties and the superpowers. The statement of general principles rather than definite terms of a settlement, however, provided a flexible frame-work of negotiation, bargaining and eventual accord. Resolution 242 was, nevertheless, an important sign of the degree of common interest that had developed between the two great powers. They had agreed to endorse the basic demands of both the parties, namely, negotiations and withdrawal, and had authorized the appointment of a special respresentative of the UN Secretary-General to facilitate a peaceful settlement.[33]

The basic objective of Soviet diplomacy during this period did not differ from the earlier period. In the words of Whetten, "Through Arab parity and restitution of Cairo's political stature, Moscow sought recognition as a major regional power and latitude commensurate with this status that would provide additional avenues for penetration and issues upon which to consolidate its presence."[34]

REFERENCES

1. Soviet interest in Syria was explained by K. Ivanov in an *Izvestia* commentary on 2 May 1966. A Tass statement published on 28 May 1966 declared that the Soviet Union "cannot and will not be indifferent to the attempts of disturbing peace in a region that is in the immediate vicinity of the borders of the Soviet Union." The Soviet Government in a note to Israel on 12 October 1966 warned it against concentrating its troops on the Syrian border. The same day, Soviet delegate Fedorenko, speaking during the debate on an Israeli complaint against Syria at the Security Council, pointed out: "Ever since the Syrian people began to consolidate their national independence and promote their social progress, military tension has begun building up on Syria's borders. We have seen that Israel has recently begun concentrating large numbers of troops along its Syrian border. Military manoeuvres have been conducted in areas near the Syrian border, and a large number of landing units equipped with artillery and minethrowers have been transferred there. Israel had partially mobilized its reserves. Furthermore, we have information that preparations are under way in Israel for an air attack on Syrian territory bordering on Israel to clear the way for incursion by Israeli forces deep into Syria." *SCOR*, 21st Year, 1307th Mtg., 14/15 October 1966, pp. 28-29.
2. A statement given by the Soviet Foreign Ministry to the Israeli Ambassador in Moscow on 26 April 1967 referred to the incident of 7 April and pointed out that the Soviet Government felt compelled to warn the Israeli government again that the risky policy Israel has been pursuing over a number of years with respect to its neighbour is "fraught with dangers, for which responsibility will fall upon the Israeli government." *Pravda/Izvestia* 27 April 1967.
3. The Soviet government's statement of 23 May 1967 clearly referred to 7 April incident and 9 May decision of the Israeli Kennesset's Committee on Foreign Policy authorizing the government to conduct military operations against Syria and subsequent movement of troops to Syrian borders. While rationalizing the Egyptian demand for the withdrawal of the UNEF as a defensive measure necessitated by the Syrian-Egyptian mutual defence pact, the statement warned : "...let no one have any doubts about the fact that should anyone try to unleash aggression in the Near East, he would be met not only with the united strength of the Arab countries but also with strong opposition to aggression from the Soviet Union and all peace-loving states." The last paragraph emphasized Soviet opposition to any breach of peace in the area ; "The Soviet Government...proceeds from the fact that the maintenance of peace and security in the area directly adjacent to the Soviet borders touches upon the vital interests of the Soviet peoples. Taking due account of the situation, the Soviet

Union is doing and will continue to do everything in its power to prevent a violation of peace and security in the Near East." *Pravda* 24 May 1967.

4. Lawrence L. Whetten, *The Canal War* (Cambridge, Mass. London, 1974), p. 36.
5. Mohamed Heikal, *Nasser, Cairo Documents* (London, New English Library. 1972), p. 219.
6. Robert Stephens, *Nasser : A Political Biography* (London, 1971), p. 484.
7. Heikal (*note 4*) p. 220.
8. L.B. Johnson, *The Vantage Point* London Delhi, 1971), pp. 295-96.
9. Walter Z. Laqueur, *The Road to War* (London, 1968), p. 160.
10. Arthur Lall, *The U.N. and the Middle East Crisis* (New York, 1968), pp. 30-31 ; see also Theodore Draper, *Israel and World Politics* (New York, 1968), pp. 80-82.
11. Jon D. Glassman, *Arms for the Arabs* (Baltimore, 1975), pp. 63-64.
12. Draper (*note* 10), p. 62.
13. *SCOR* 22nd Year, 1342nd Mtg., 24 May 1967, p. 9.
14. *Ibid.*, 134rd Mtg., 29 May 1967, p. 22.
15. *SWB* Pt. I, 5-6 June 1967.
16. *Facts-on-File*, XXXVII, 1967, p. 186.
17. Whetten (*note* 4), p. 43. The Egyptian leadership itself was convinced that the closure of the Straits will make the war a hundred per cent certainty. See Anwar el-Sadat, *In Search of Identity* (London, 1978), pp. 172-173.
18. Johnson (*note* 8), pp. 287-289.
19. *Ibid.*, p. 298.
20. *Pravda*, 8 June 1967.
21. *Pravda*, 10 June 1967.
22. Johnson (*note* 8), p· 302.
23. Israeli General Haim Bar Lev later confirmed in an interview that American pressure had been the determining factor in halting Israeli forces before they could attack Damascus. *New Middle East*, March 1971, p. 37.
24. Whetten (*note* 4), p. 44.
25. *Pravda*, 11 June 1967.
26. *Pravda/Izvestia*, 22 June 1967.
27. *GAOR*, V ES Session, 1967, 1526th Mtg., 19 June 1967, pp. 3-6.
28. *Ibid.*, p. 6.
29. Gideon Rafael, "UN Resolution 242 : A Common Denominator". *New middle East*, June 1973.
30. *SMB* Pt I, 9 September 1967 ; 13 September 1967.
31. *Department of the State Bulletin* 57 (1463), 10 July 1967, pp. 37-38.
32. The Soviet draft analysed in Lall (*note* 10), pp. 255-59.
33. Resolution 242 (1967) reads as follows :
"*The Security Council,*

Expressing its continuing concern with the grave situation in the Middle East,

Emphasizing the inadmissibility of the acquisition of territory by war and the need to work for a just and lasting peace in which every state in the area can live in security,

Emphasizing further that all member states in their acceptance of the Charter of the United Nations have undertaken a commitment to act in accordance with Article 2 of the Charter,

1. *Affirms* that the fulfilment of Charter principles requires the establishment of a just and lasting peace in the Middle East which should include the application of both the following principles :

   (i) Withdrawal of Israeli armed forces from territories occupied in the recent conflict ;

   (ii) Termination of all claims or states of belligerency and respect for and acknowledgement of the sovereignty, territorial integrity, and political independence of every state in the area and their right to' live in peace within secure and recognized boundaries free from threats or acts of force ;

2. *Affirms further* the necessity

   (a) for guaranteeing freedom of navigation through international waterways in the area ;

   (b) for achieving a just settlement of the refugee problem ;

   (c) for guaranteeing the territorial inviolability and political independence of every state in the area, through measures including the establishment of demilitarized zones ;

3. *Requests* the Secretary-General to designate a special representative to proceed to the Middle East to establish and maintain contacts with the states concerned in order to promote agreement and assist efforts to achieve a peaceful and accepted settlement in accordance with the provisions and principles in this resolution ;

4. *Requests* the Secretary-General to the Security Council on the progress of the efforts to of the special representative as soon as possible."

   Adopted unanimously at the 1382nd meeting, 22 November 1967.

34. Whetten (*note* 4), p. 363.

CHAPTER V

Diplomatic Stalemate 1968-1972

Soviet Diplomatic Offensive

Although Soviet prestige had suffered a lot during the War of June 1967, the consequences of the war, far from eliminating Soviet influence from the area, ensured the psychological, diplomatic and strategic dependence of the vanquished upon the Soviet Union. For the first time since their rapprochement with the Arab East the Soviets were compelled to formulate a consistent and coherent policy towards the Arab-Israeli conflict. No longer was the conflict seen by the Soviets, as the Western powers saw it, as a clash of two local nationalisms which was better to be resolved locally. The Soviet Union commit itself to rehabilitating and consolidating the defensive capability of the "progressive" Arab states because it now looked at the Arab struggle against Israel as a just struggle against imperialism and the Arab revolutionary movement as an integral part of the world historical revolutionary process. The first step towards this direction was taken even during the course of the June War when the Soviet Union threatened to intervene to prevent the collapse of the Syrian regime in face of an advancing Israeli army. The second step was taken by instituting a programme of military and economic assistance to the victims of aggression and by forging an anti-imperialist Arab coalition. "Rendering extensive aid to the Arab peoples in their struggle against imperialist aggression," wrote a Soviet commentator in the wake of the June War, "the Soviet Union promotes the world revolutionary process. The interests that have clashed in the Middle East are not narrow national inteserts of individual countries; the Middle East has become an arena of a struggle between the forces of progress and reaction, peace and war, socialism and imperialism. The Soviet Union is fulfilling the internationalist duty in the Middle East."[1] In a political sense, this amount to a dynamic policy of the penetration of the Arab East by ensuring a regional balance so that the Arab States could negotiate a settlement from a position of equality. The anchor sheet of this policy was the explicit Soviet commitment to a *political*, rather than a military settlement of thc conflict and distraction of the sponsored states from military adventures which could lead to newer wars and invite superpower intervention. With a view to consolidating their influence in the longer term, the Soviets insisted on the stationing of Soviet military advisers in the sponsored states and tried in a later period to gain control over the decision-making process in these states by concluding treaties of friendship and cooperation. However, the greatest obstacle in the way of consolidation and expansion of Soviet influence in the area was the American policy of ensuring a regional balance in which Israeli military was superior to the combined armed forces of all the Arab states. The United States has seen the Soviet actions in the area from 1967 to 1973 as a direct threat to American interests and influence. The containment and/or elimination of Soviet influence has been, despite the progress towards detente and the two-power and four-power talks for a regional settlement during 1969-1972, and implicit objective of American policy. The United States really wanted a settlement but under its own auspices. Thus, if no breakthrough could be achieved during this period it was because the Arab-Israeli conflict had become a surrogate of the Soviet-American competition for influence and became Israeli sabotaged the Jarring mission.

The initial efforts at promoting a political settlement having failed by October 1968, the Soviet Union had no option but to acquiesce in the Egyptian decision to launch a "war of Attrition" against the Israeli forces entrenched on the east bank of the Suez Canal, as a helpful supplement to its peace diplomacy. It provided the Soviet Union with an opportunity to draw the attention of the great powers and the world community to the dangerous situation in the area and to press them to facilitate a settlement. Soviet intervention in the crisis of 1970 arising out of Israeli deep-penetration raids into the Egyptian heartland, was the high-water mark of the Soviet commitment to the preservation of the pro-Soviet regimes. But Soviet aim was strictly defensive and so it ensured a military stalemate in which Israel was unable to overrun the Arab countries. This statement of 'no peace, no war' was quite in tune with the growing detente between the two superpowers. The realization of this statements and diplomatic immobilism on the part of the superpowers was mainly responsible for developing strain in Soviet-Egyptian relations which led to lhe expulsion of Soviet military advisers from Egypt in July 1972 and independent decision by Egypt to prepare for the War.

The operation rehabilitation which was launched by the Soviet Union soon after the debacle of June 1967 quickly restored the Egyptian and Syrian armies to their pre-war potential. In return, the Soviet Union got naval and air facilities in these countries and appeared to have induced a pro-Soviet orientation in their foreign policies. Simultaneous with military aid and training, a concerted propaganda campaign was launched during the first half of 1968 through the Soviet media against continuing Israeli military operations and Israeli designs for the captured Arab territories. An *Izvestia* article published on 15 January, referring to the communique issued after Eshkol-Johnson meeting promised sympathetic consideration of the Israeli request for arms, pointed out that the United States was interested "not in the mere annexation of Arab territory by Israeli invaders" but she would also like Israel "to become the stronghold of American strategic and economic influence in the Middle East so that American monopolies could consolidate their oil positions there."[2] Another article in *Pravda* of 6 March alluded to hypocritical statements of Israeli leaders about their readiness for talks and at the same time referring to the occupied areas as "enemy" territory. "In the actions of the Israeli ruling circles", it concluded, "the world public rightly sees the desire to torpedo the Jarring mission, to make still another dangerous step along the adventurist way."[3] The Soviet government published a detailed statement on West Asia on 23 March, presaging its coming dialogue with the Egyptian and American governments, which noted the escalation of tension by Israel, firmly committed itself to a political solution and liquidation of the consequences of Israeli aggression and expressed its determination to go on aiding the victims of aggression.[4] During the Security Council's debate on a recent Israeli raid into Jordan, the USSR representative called for sanctions against the aggressor.[5] Primakov on 24 May noted that "By rejecting the Security Council Resolution and by torpedoing the mission of Jarring, the Tel Aviv leaders have completely unmasked themselves and have come forth as open oppents to peace in the Middle East. This is the only way one can appraise Israel's actions."[6] Soviet opposition to a reported plan attributed to Israeli deputy premier Yigal Allon, regarding a territorial settlement with Jordan providing for annexation of East Jerusalem and areas north and south of it to Israel, was voiced in *Izvestia* of 19 June.[7] During July and August the Soviet Union was preoccupied with problems created by the liberalization movement in Czechoslovakia. But although this question dominated the Soviet media till the end of the year, the Soviets were able to switch their attention to West Asia soon after their occupation of Czechoslovakia.

Towards the end of 1968, the Soviet Union was confronted with a dilemma in its Arab policy. How to reconcile the need to prevent violence in the area with the need to pacify the

Arabs ? In the aftermath of the disastrous June War, the Soviets had indicated to the Arabs that the only practical solution to the crisis was one achieved through political means. They would not allow a war of liberation which resulted in yet another Arab defeat or loss of prestige to the Soviet Union or invited direct superpower confrontation. However, owing to the miraculous morale-boosting effect of the Soviet military aid it was no longer possible to pacify the Arab public opinion which now demanded concrete action instead of diplomatic rhetoric. If the Soviet Union continued to stress the political method it might antagonize and alienate the radicals but if it left the field to the war party it would amount to her abdication from the West Asian arena. Meanwhile, the conflict level had progressively risen from June 1968 to the launching of the Egyptian war of attrition in May-June 1969 which resulted in the collapse of Egyptian defences necessitating the direct assumption by the Soviet Union of the responsibility of the aerial defence of Egypt against Israeli strategic bombings. It is against this background that the Soviet diplomatic offiensive was launched with the sole purpose of putting maximum international pressure on Israel to withdraw from the occupied Arab areas and thus pacify the Arabs. Soviet peace diplomacy involved two-power and four-power consultations for a regional settlement and its most tangible products were the Rogers' peace plans I and II.

This Soviet diplomatic offensive appears to have been launched with a sharp Tass statement denouncing Israeli military operations against Egypt in violation of the ceasefire agreement and referred to the Israeli raid of 31 October 1968 on the Nag Hammadi power station which demonstrated the vulnerability of the Aswan High Dam (a monument of the Soviet economic aid to the third world) to Israeli air strikes. The statement acknowledged the Arab readiness for a peaceful settlement of the conflict and hinted at the situation getting out of control : "It is the duty of all peace-loving states to prevent another dangerous explosion in the region."[8] A *Pravda* leader on 3 December again emphasized the need for preventing a "dangerous explosion" in the region and pointed out that the UN Security Council's Resolution of 22 November, 1967 and the Egyptian proposal to implement it in stages provided a "realistic basis" for peace. The joint communique issued after Soviet Foreign Minister Andrei Gromyko's visit to Cairo from 21 to 24 December reaffirmed Egypt's commitment to the political settlement line.[9] This was followed up by a formal Soviet note to the USA on 30 December in which the Soviet government outlined its peace plan (within the framework of the UN Security Council Resolution of 22 November 1967), main points of which were published in a *pravda* article on 25 January 1969. In later years, the Soviet Union kept on presenting variations upon this initial line in accordance with the requirements of political bargaining. By the time the Soviet Union succeeded in establishing a viable military stalemate on the Suez Canal front to deter Israel from attacking Egypt, it had also exhausted all diplomatic efforts to procure a political settlement and had gone to the extreme of accepting most of the Israeli-American demands in exchange of a time-bound, phased withdrawal of Israeli forces from the occupied areas.[10] As a matter of fact, both Rogers' peace plans were the outcome of the behind-the-scene Soviet-American cooperation. The Soviet diplomatic offensive drew a blank because of Israel's obstinacy and absence of real American pressure on her to make concessions. The stumbling block in the way of a peaceful settlement seemed to be the American policy of ensuring a regional balance in which Israel enjoyed superiority over the combined military strength of all the Arab states. In a statement published in the *New York Times* of 8 May 1969 Israeli Premier Golda Meir said that Israel could not be expected to return the strategic areas captured in 1967. She described the four-power talks as "interference" in the affairs of small states and insisted on direct negotiations between the belligerents and a negotiated settlement. In its reply to Jarring's Aide-Memoire of 8 February 1971 the Israel government categorically declared that it would not withdraw its forces to the pre-June 1967 borders. Meir later noted in her autobiography that she repeatedly explained to Rogers that "such a compromise (among great powers) might satisfy the demand of US-Soviet detente but it would certainly not result in any binding guarantees for Israel's safety."[11]

Four-Power Talks and Rogers' Plan I

The Soviet Union appeared to have solid reasons for resorting to informal, behind-the-scene two power and four-power consultations at the United Nations headquarters within the framework of UN Security Council Resolution 242. First, her participation in big-power consultations contained lesser risks than in a fresh regional hot war fraught with risky liabilities. Second, the Soviet Union was equally apprehensive of both Arab extremism and Israeli expansionism. By involving the great powers in a discussion of the regional problems it sought to introduce a sort of an external check on the local powers. Third, since the Soviet Union by committing itself to the Arab side ever since the war of 1967 had become deeply involved in the Arab-Israeli conflict it had to convince the Arab public of the utility of the Soviet line and mobilize it behind it by showing that progress was possible through the concert of big powers and/or the United Nations. Fourth, just as during the war of 1967, it was now also motivated by the desire of avoiding superpower confrontation in regional disputes. And finally, the Soviet Union was anxious to expand the detente and understanding with the USA in the larger interest of mutually beneficial cooperation. Ever since the passage of UN Security Resolution of 22 November 1967 the USSR and and USA were interpreting it differently. While the USSR visualized a comprehensive package settlement involving the simultaneous implementation of all parts of the said resolution, the USA regarded the resolution merely as a framework and a point of departure, insisting on a piecemeal approach to a settlement leading to territorial adjustments for secure and recognized borders. The USSR now tried to bridge these differences and find common grounds with its adversary towards a settlement which had become indispensable for the consolidation of its influence in the region. The initial exchange of notes between the USSR and USA in December 1968—January 1969 provided an opportunity to explore the two rival positions to eliminate common grounds.[12]

The idea of four-power consultations was picked up by the Soviet Union from France.[13] After initial consultation between the representatives of the two superpowers the UN delegate of the Big Four started their joint deliberations on 4 April 1969.[14] After the failure of the two Rogers' peace plans and Israeli rejection of the joint Soviet-American offer of four-power guarantees of Israel's frontiers, the USA suspended these negotiations and resorted to a unilateral initiative to explore the possibility of at least a partial settlement in the Suez Canal Zone, which could not materialize due to the exclusion of the Soviet Union and Egyptian rejection of the idea.[15] An analysis of the various proposals for a regional settlement presented by the Soviet Union during this phase reflect certain basic features, namely, that (1) prior consultations with Cairo and Damascus before advancing any bargaining position was almost an article of faith for the Soviet Union. It seemed to have identified itself completely with the major Arab demand for total withdrawal of Israeli forces from the occupied Arab areas as a precondition to any settlement. (2) The Soviet Union did not submit itself to the American-Israeli demand for territorial rectifications towards demarcation of "recognized and secure" borders. (3) The Soviet Union in compliance with the Arab wishes consistently refused to accept the Israeli demand for direct negotiations resulting in a peace treaty. (When finally the Soviets joined hands with the USA in calling for direct negotiations between the belligerents to implement Resolution 242 through Resolution 338 of the UN Security Council on 22 October 1973, it was because the vanquished of 1967 had demonstrated their equality with the victors in the battlefield of 1973 and there no longer existed the fear of capitulation by either party). (4) The Soviet Union consistently rejected the American proposal (publicly) for limiting arms supplies to the region to freeze the conflict, saying that it was inconceivable so long as Israeli forces were occupying Arab territories. And finally, the Soviet Union would not accept an American-sponsored initiative which undercut the longer-term Soviet strategic political interest in the area. This last point needs elaboration in light of Soviet reaction to the American peace proposals presented by the US Secretary of State William P. Rogers on 28 October 1969.[16]

Rogers' peace plan I (which called for the withdrawal of Israeli forces from occupied Arab lands in return of Arab recognition of Israeli's territorial integrity) was in fact a product of joint deliberations at New York between US Assistant Secretary of State Joseph Sisco and Soviet Ambassador to the US Anatoli Dobrynin. These proposals brightened the chance of a breakthrough as the Arab-Soviet side had tacitly agreed to the 1949 Rhodes-type formula of proximity talks between the parties through the good offices of Gunnar Jarring. Although the Soviet side had co-authored the plan, it refrained from cosponsoring it even though some of the key elements of the Soviet peace plan were incorporated into it, namely, the idea of a time-table for Israeli withdrawal, the repatriation of the refugee or their resettlement outside Israel with compensation, and the Rhodes formula for proximity talks.[17] Israel rejected these proposals immediately by insisting that proximity talks should be construed as direct talks. It sabotaged it to prevent an American rapprochement with the Arab states. Israeli rejection entailed Egyptian rejection. The Soviet Union had its own after-thought to go back on its previous understanding with the USA. In a Soviet note given to the US Department of State 23 December 1969 the proposals were criticized point-by-point and rejected : (i) the American proposals were pro-Israel and onesided : (ii) direct negotiations or Rhodes-style talks cannot take place before Israeli withdrawal is effected ; (iii) nothing concrete has been offered to the Palestinian refugees. Israel would have to fulfil all previous UN resolutions on the repatriation of the refugees; and that mere shifting of the centre of gravity from fourpower talks to produce a settlement to a reactivation of the Jarring mission to produce it will not produce any result.[18]

The Americans in moving the Rogers' proposals and the Soviets in rejecting them were motivated by their own self-interest. That the plan was a political move aimed at softening the Arab attitudes towards the United States is testified by Nixon : "I knew that Rogers' plan could never be implemented, but I believed that it was important to let the Arab world know that the United States did not automatically dismiss its case regarding the occupied territories or rule out a compromise settlement of the conflicting claims. With the Rogers' plan on the record, I thought it would be easier for the Arab leaders to propose reopening relations with the United States without coming under attack from the hawks and pro-Soviet elements in their own countries."[19] The Soviets did not wish to arrange for the normalization of relations between the USA and the Soviet-backed states. They also wanted a temporary suspension of the two-power talks to engage their attention with the regional arena where Israel's deep penetration raids into Egypt had torn the balance of power into pieces. The Soviet Union intervened in the crisis of 1970 with all the resources available to it to redress the regional balance and the diplomatic offensive was not resumed till after the coming into being of the temporary ceasefire arranged under Rogers' peace plan II on 7 August 1970.

Soviet Intervention in the Crisis of 1970

Was the "War of Attrition" of Egyptian making or a Soviet inspired war ? Why did the the Soviets choose to support this war ? Finally, what led them to assume, for the first time in their history, the direct responsibility for the aerial defence of a country which lay outside the socialist community ? The answers to these questions illuminate the longer-term Soviet interest in the region.

The War of Attrition was announced by President Nasser on his own initiative on 1 April 1969 and effectively implemented from 20 July onwards. It came to an end with the American-sponsored ceasefire on 7 August 1970. Although sporadic fighting had broken out several times on the Suez Canal front since June 1967, it was the first concerted and sustained Egyptian offensive against Israeli fortified positions on the east bank of the Suez Canal to break their morale and force them to withdraw from the Sinai. It was directed at breaking the stalemate of "no war, no peace" which had been legalized through the UN-sponsored ceasefire. The immediate purpose of this offensive seemed to prevent the conversion of the Suez Canal into a *de facto* boundary between Egypt and Israel. But the ultimate and avowed purpose was to force Israel's withdrawal from the Suez Canal or acceptance by her of a political settlement acceptable to Egypt. The Israelis responded by using their superior air power to pound the fortified infantry on the west bank but failed to check the

Egyptian offensive. The continuing relative success of the War of Attrition forced the Israeli leadership to choose between political negotiations or an alternative military strategy to defeat the Egyptian offensive. The Israelis opted for the American strategy of deep-penetration bombing into the enemy heartland which had successfully operated against North Vietnam. In January 1970 the Israeli air force began to deploy its newly acquired American F-4 Phantom fighter-bombers first to destroy Egyptian air defence and then to attack military, civilian and economic targets deep inside Egypt to break the morale of the Egyptian people and topple the regime of President Nasser. (According to the *Strategic Survey* 1971, [London, 1972], the Israeli air force had flown 3,300 sorties and dropped 8000 tons of ordnance on the Egyptian territory during the first four months of 1970). The Israelis by their successful counter-offensive offered President Nasser a choice between ignominious defeat or capitulation on Israeli terms. But President Nasser sought another alternative : to continue the war of attrition with active Soviet support and defence cover.

The Soviet leadership was taken aback by the turn of events against Egypt and Egyptian heavy losses due to Israel's deep-penetration raids. In a statement read on behalf of the Soviet Foreign Ministry by L.M. Zamyatin on 31 October, the Soviet government reminded of the consistent Soviet line of seeking a peaceful settlement compatible with the UN decisions and reiterated that the Soviet Union will "continue to extend comprehensive aid to the Arab states struggling for national independence, for the maintenance of the progressive gains of their peoples against the encroachment of Israel and its imperialist protectors...."[20]. Another statement issued on behalf of six European socialist countries on -7 November decried the imperialist attempt to topple the progressive regimes in the area and assured every assistance to the Arab states.[21] Then Premier Kosygin declared on 10 December at a luncheon given to the visiting official delegation from Egypt that as long as Israel's aggression continued the Soviet Union would pursue "active measures to strengthen the defence capacity of the UAR and other Arab states."[22] The Soviet Union also turned down repeated American suggestion during this period for an arms embargo in the area on the ground that it would be inconceivable so long as Israel was in possession of the Arab lands.[23] These verbal expressions of support did not deter Israel. Then President Nasser went on a secret mission to Moscow on 22 January 1970 to request the Soviet leaders to intervene more effectively and assume the direct responsibility of the aerial defence of Egypt. According to Heikal,[24] who accompanied Nasser on the mission, the Soviet leaders were reluctant to intervene directly but when Nasser threatened to resign, they promised to consider the Egyptian request to consider measures to protect Egypt from Israeli raids.

The Soviet Union then sent a note to the governments of the USA, Britain and France on 31 January 1970 in which it laid the blame for worsening of the situation in the region on American supplies of latest and sophisticated weapons and aeroplanes to Israel. Egypt was virtually defenceless against Israeli Phantoms which were attacking at will. "We would like to tell you in all frankness," the note concluded, "that if Israel continues its adventurism, to bomb the territory of the UAR and of other states, *the Soviet Union will be forced to see to it that the Arab states have means at their disposal, with the help of which a due rebuff to the arrogant aggressor could be made*."[25] (emphasis added).

It was the rather savage and devastating bombing of a steel mill at Abu Za'bal in the vicinity of Cairo on 12 February at the beginning of the working day when about 1,800 workers had assembled there, killing two hundred of them, that forced the hands of the Soviet leaders. Tass reported on 16 February that the Soviet Union would provide the Arabs with "necessary support" to strengthen their defences against Israeli attacks, strongly implying that a decision to supply advanced defensive weapons to Egypt had been taken.[26]

When the four-power talks were resumed on 19 February, the American side reiterated its proposals of 28 October 1969 which had already been rejected by Egypt and the USSR. With the Abu Za'bal incident fresh in mind and the seeming reluctance of the USA to restrain Israel, the Soviet side had no option but to turn down the American proposal for a ceasefire-in-place without a prior commitment by Israel to the principle of withdrawal of its forces from Arab territory. Soviet representative Jacob Malik also rejected the American call for an arms embargo in the region and asserted that while the United States was supplying Israel with advanced offensive weapons which had created an imbalance, the Soviet Union was giving only defensive weapons to the Arabs. The impasse in the two-power talks left the Soviet Union with no alternative but to seek its own remedies to redress the balance.[27] From the end of February the Soviet Union inducted new types of aircraft and missile and personnel to handle them which neutralized the Israeli superiority in the air. During the coming two years the Soviet Union erected a formidable system of the aerial defence of the entire Nile Valley.[28] The strength of Soviet personnel in Egypt was believed to be around 20,000.

On 13 April, Israeli aircraft raiding deep into Egypt were intercepted by a formation of Mig-21s reportedly manned by Soviet pilots. On making contact, the Israeli planes retreated and thereafter deep-penetration raids came to an end. Although the period from May onwards was marked by the concentration of Soviet attention on developments in Indo-China, particularly American intervention in Cambodia and Laos, the Soviets did not remain indifferent to West Asia. A Tass statement of 30 May tersely denounced the Israeli invasion of southern Lebanon.[29] During May and June the Egyptians succeeded with the Soviet help in pushing their air defence system towards the Suez Canal. Soviet intervention had forced Israel to accept ceasefire and resumption of talks under Jarring as arranged under Rogers' Plan II. However, Israel sabotaged the talks by its negative attitude and hurt the susceptibilities of the USSR as a superpower by attacking the Soviet forces in the Canal Zone prior to the ceasefire of 7 August. It paid the price in the form of extension of the air defence system along the entire west bank of the Canal.

It has been asked whether the War of Attrition was an Egyptian-planned war or inspired by the USSR as charged by Golda Meir.[30] In retrospect, it appears to be an Egyptian-planned war necessitated by the growing domestic and regional pressures on Egypt, mounting economic difficulties, rising defence expenditure, and dim prospects of a political settlement.

The USSR, which was committed to a consistent policy of preventing war and seeking a political settlement in terms of Resolution 242, and was earnestly trying to bring about a settlement promulgated by the four powers and guaranteed by them, had no way except acquiescing in the Egyptian decision to launch a limited offensive. But once it got momentum the Soviets might have considered it as a helpful supplement to their diplomatic bargaining with the other powers.

Soviet intervention in this crisis does not appear to be motivated by any desire to escalate regional tensions or corner Israel and America but by the complexities of the regional situation created by Israeli strategic bombing, posing a threat to the survival of President Nasser's regime. The Soviets did not come in at their own will: they were invited by the Egyptian leadership to rescue Egypt from an impossible situation. Soviet intervention was, thus, of a *defensive*, not *offensive* character. It was meant to be essentially a "rescue operation". Ever since mid-1950s Egypt had been the beachead for Soviet advances in the area and the collapse of Nasser's regime would entail not only loss of prestige but also negation of the massive investment made in military and economic aid over a decade. It might also have been, as Rubenstein has surmised, a function of Soviet domestic politics. Those among the Soviet leadership who despite the Arab defeat in 1967 had defended the Soviet forward policy in the region "could not shy away from securing that policy without leaving themselves vulnerable to attack from opponents in the leadership."[31]

In sum, keeping in view the global and regional balance of power, it is inconceivable that the USSR desired a general war in the area. It stepped in simply to redress the regional balance which had seriously been disturbed by Israel backed by America. The Soviet Union appeared to have set the outer limit of its commitment to the defence of the Nile Valley only ; it would not underwrite an Egyptian war of liberation. It would rather withdraw from Egypt in July 1972 than to become a party to Egypt's war against Israel. Its self-restraint was visible not only during this crisis but also the coming crisis in Jordan where Syrian forces had gone in September to intervene on behalf of the beleagured Palestinians. America had threatened intervention with physical force to halt Syrian intervention in Jordan. The Soviets chose to keep silence over the liquidation of the Palestinian guerillas by the Jordanian army and in a note to Washington on 18 September assured that they had no intention of intervening in Jordan. Subsequently they pressed Syria to withdraw its forces from Jordan.[32]

The Soviets supported Rogers' peace plan II aiming at a limited 90-day ceasefire and resumption of peace talks under Jarring. They encouraged the Arabs to accept the ceasefire and cooperate with Jarring. In the wake of Israeli-American allegations of violation of the August ceasefire by Egypt and the USSR, Soviet government emphasized that the basic issue was not any alleged violations of the ceasefire but to get the talks started. In a Soviet Foreign Ministry statement published on 9 October, the Soviet Union reaffirmed its commitment to a political settlement by all possible means.[33]

Rogers' Plan II and Ceasefire

Soviet intervention in the crisis of 1970 and assumption of the direct responsibility of the aerial defence of the Egyptian mainland had deterred Israel from aggression against Egypt. At the same time, it created the possibility of greater escalation on the Suez Canal front. The United States initially responded by selling more strategic war-planes to Israel and adopting a bellicose posture towards the Soviet Union. However, in order to halt further Soviet advances in the area, to forestall a major confrontation between the local powers involving their superpower patrons, and to open a new chapter in American-Arab relations, Washington was compelled to rethink its policy and whittle down its proposals of 28 October 1969 to a two-point plan announced on 19 June for a 90-day ceasefirc followed by resumption of negotiations under Jarring to implement Resolution 242.[34] Certain developments which inclined the USA to reopen its peace initiative were : Realization by the parties of a stalemate on the Suez Canal front ; President Nasser's May Day speech that year which asked for an even-handed

American policy in the Arab-Israeli conflict ; Nasser's statement on 14 June that he might consider a ceasefire in six months or less ; and Mrs Meir's acceptance in principle of Resolution 242 with all its implications. According to Heikal, there were three reasons behind the American initiative : failure of the Israeli offensive against the Nile Valley ; reinforcement of the Egyptian army ; and increased Soviet aid.[35] President Nasser went to Moscow on 29 June to consult with the Soviet leaders about the latest American plan. The Soviet leaders expressed their desire for a settlement based on Resolution 242 "with due account for the legitimate rights and interests of all peoples in the area, including Israel."[36]

Nasser accepted the Rogers plan without any reservations on 22 July. Jordanian acceptance followed on 27 July. Syria did not accept it. It embarrassed Israel which delayed its acceptance till 31 July, then its last-minute reservations delayed the ceasefire till 7 August.

The acceptance of the American initiative by Egypt and Israel was a turning-point in the history of the Arab-Israeli conflict. It is not clear yet whether the Soviets persuaded Nasser to accept the Rogers plan or it was Nasser who persuaded the Soviets to give their consent to his personal decision. Nasser had gambled in the dark by accepting a ceasefire without a prior Israeli commitment to the withdrawal of its forces or to the peace negotiations. On the other hand, Israeli acceptance implied a crumbling of the three pillars of Israeli foreign policy since June 1967 : her demand for direct negotiations with the Arabs ; her rejection of the term "withdrawal" from the occupied areas ; and an official non-commitment to carry out all the provisions of Resolution 242. The decision was made only after intense pressure from America accompanied by assurances and guarantees.

Opinions differ regarding what determined the Egyptian decision to accept the Rogers Plan. Some like Glassman[37] imply that it was mainly a result of Soviet pressure. But others like Sadat and Heikal[38] indicate that it was primarily an Egyptian decision with which the USSR complied. However, as Rubenstein says "though Moscow did not initiate the diplomatic process nor dictate to Nasser the decision culminating in the ceasefire of August 7, it did apparently use some leverage to encourage his acceptance of the Rogers Plan."[39] Nasser might have been inclined to use the American lever to force an Israeli withdrawal and the Soviets encouraged this by further promises of arms aid.

That the USSR adopted a positive and supportive attitude towards the American initiative is illustrated by a speech of Communist Party General Secretary, Leonid Brezhnev delivered on 28 August at Alma Ata : "The Soviet Union, naturally, takes a positive view of this development of events. Our country has always insisted that Gunnar Jarring's mission, which was entrusted to him by the Security Council, should be carried out fully and effectively" and that "It is in the general interests of peoples to do everything possible for a settlement of the Middle East conflict and for the present ceasefire to become a good beginning for a just, firm and lasting peace in the Middle East ..."[40] Contradicting the allegations of violation of the ceasefire by Egypt and USSR, Soviet Foreign Ministry statement on 8 October declared "The Soviet Union did not take part in drafting any of the ceasefire terms in the Suez Canal zone. These terms were put forward by the American side. For its part, aware of the great importance of this step, the Soviet Union from the very outset consistently advocated a ceasefire and did everything in its power to facilitate the mission of Dr. Jarring, through whose mediation the sides were to start an exchange of views."[41]

The record of Soviet diplomacy from July 1970 to March 1971, when bilateral talks with the USA were suspended, in delivering the Arabs to the bargaining table and its readiness to join other big powers in guaranteeing the boundaries in West Asia, shows that the Soviet Union worked wholeheartedly for a peaceful accord. There is truth in Whetten's assertion that "The second Rogers plan was in reality a Soviet product and its failure was largely Israel's responsibility."[42] Israel, alleging violations of the ceasefire, refused to participate in talks through Jarring and when the mission was revived in January 1971 Israel challenged Jarring's right to act as a mediator. Thereupon, Jarring suspended his mission indefinitely in April. President Nasser died suddenly on 28 September. His successor, Anwar Sadat, renewed the ceasefire for a second term and only for a month for the third time.

That the Soviet Union was committed to a policy of seeking a political settlement is beyond doubt. The failure of that policy is attributable not to any logical flaw in its formulation but to the nature of superpower competition for influence of which the regional conflict in West Asia became a surrogate. By following a policy of polarization in the area hitherto, the USSR had restricted its influence to one of the belligerents. It could deter the other but could not force it to make diplomatic concessions.[43] (That became eventually one of the reasons for the coming of pax Americana in the Egyptian-Israeli sector).

Search for an Interim Settlement

In a dramatic peace initiative on 4 February 1971, President Sadat announced that Egypt would extend the ceasefire for one month to 7 March. Earlier he had taken the hard line of not renewing the ceasefire for another term unless Israel presented a time-table for the withdrawal of its forces. He also proposed to reopen the Suez Canal on condition that Israeli troops made a partial withdrawal from the east bank as a first step towards a final withdrawal to the former mandate borders.[44] The move was enthusiastically received in Washington. But Israel's terms for a partial settlement were radically different from those of Egypt. In the wake of the recent Suez and Jordanian crises and failure of the four-power talks, the United States decided to play a mediatory role for bringing about at least a partial interim settlement resulting in the reopening of the Suez Canal. On 29 March Rogers presented to Egypt and Israel a plan to reopen the Canal. From 1-8 May he visited four Arab states and Israel. It was the first visit by an American Secretary of State to Egypt since 1953.

However, it was not the terms of an interim accord that caused the demise of the initiative but Israel's insistence that the accord be regarded not as an interim but a separate accord unrelated to a general peace settlement in the area. This was not acceptable to Egypt. Meanwhile, in an attempt to break the deadlock, Donald Bergus, an American representative in Cairo, reportedly presented to Egyptian Foreign Minister Mahmoud Riad a memorandum suggesting an Israeli withdrawal across half the Sinai in exchange for a protracted ceasefire. The Bergus idea flopped as Riad made it public prematurely thus creating a sort of a crisis of confidence between Israel and the USA.

The Soviets became alarmed at the American initiative for a partial accord and hobnobbing of the Americans with Egyptian officials. Heikal, in the wake of the so-called Bergus affairs thought that America genuinely wanted a solution for the region provided it was an American solution.[45] Meanwhile, the internal leadership crisis in Egypt resulting in the liquidation of the pro-Soviet elements from Egyptian government and party, forced the hands of the Soviet leaders. President Nikolai Podgorny came with the draft of a friendship and cooperation treaty. By signing the treaty on 28 May 1971 Egypt parted company with America. In this period Soviet commentators continued to criticize the Rogers' moves as attempes to create dissension among the Arab states and create a wedge between them and the Soviet Union.[46]

Disappointed over the failure of the American initiative, Egypt fell back on Soviet support which was now assured through a formal treaty. From October 1971 through January 1972 the United States continued its attempts to make Israel agree to a precise formula for a partial accord. Finally, when Golda Meir accepted the American proposal for proximity talks, Sadat was searching a new approach to end the deadlock—preparation for a war—and ostensibly with that aim in view he visited Moscow on 2 February 1972.

REFERENCES

1. V. Kudryavtsev, "The Middle East Knot". *International Affairs* (9), September 1967, pp. 33-34. See also V. Lykov, "Middle East : No Time to Lose". *New Times* (13), 31 March 1970.
2. *Daily Review*, 16 January 1968.
3. *Ibid.*, 6 March 1968.
4. *Pravda*, 23 March 1968.
5. Radio Moscow in Arabic, 27 March 1968/*SWB*/Pt. I, 27 March 1968.

6. *Daily Review*, 24 May 1968.
7. *Ibid.*, 20 June 1968.
8. *Pravda/Izvestia*, 7 November 1968.
9. Tass, 24 December 1968.
10. See Chapter VII of this work.
11. *Golda Meir, My Life* (London, 1975), p. 320.
12. *New York Times*, 21 January 1969.
13. *Cf. Mizan*, 11 (1), January-February 1969, pp. 3-7.
14. *SWB/I*, 6 January 1969 : *Keesing's Contemporary Archives*, 12 (1969-70), pp. 23325, 23669.
15. Perhaps the most authoritative account of the four-power consultations and military developments during this period is found in Lawrence L. Whetten, *The Canal War* (Cambridge Mass/London, 1974), pp. 71-161.
16. See Gromyko's statement in *GAOR*, 24th Session, 1756th Mtg., 19 September 1969, pp. 9-10.
17. Unofficial text in *New York Times*, 22 December 1969.
18. Excerpts published in a commentary published in *Pravda*, 14 January 1970.
19. Richard M. Nixon, *Memoirs* (New York, 1978), p. 479.
20. *Pravda*, 1 November 1969.
21. *Pravda* 27 November 1967.
22. *Pravda* 11 December 1969 ; *Keesing's* 17 (1970), p. 23817.
23. See *GAOR*, 25th Session, 1890th Mtg., 29 October 1970, pp. 8-9.
24. Mohamed Heikal, *The Road To Ramadan* (London, 1975), pp. 83-88 ; Anwar el-Sadat, *In Search of Identity* (London, 1978), pp. 197-198.
25. The *Times* 5 February 1970 ; Nixon (*note* 19), p. 479.
26. *Pravda* 17 February 1970.
27. Whetten (*note* 15), p. 4.
28. *The Strategic Survey*, 1970 (London, 1971, pp. 46-49) estimated the market value of the Soviet military equipment supplied to Egypt since the 1967 war as having increased during 1970 from 2,000 million to 4,500 million dollars. By the end of October, some 500-600 SAM launchers had been established along the Canal, about 200 of them being located within 19 miles of the ceasefire line. The forward element of the new system permitted coverage of an area extending 12 miles into the Israeli occupied Sinai Peninsula.
29. *Daily Review*, 1 June 1970.
30. Meir (*note* 11), pp. 319-320.
31. Alvin Z. Rubenstein, *Red Star on the Nile* (Princeton, 1977), p. 110.
32. Nixon (*note* 19), pp. 483-84.
33. *Pravda*, 9 October 1970.
34. Texts in the *Department of State Bulletin*, 10 August 1970, pp. 178-179.
35. *New Middle East*, September 1970, pp. 27-29.

36. Tass, 30 June 1970.
37. John D. Glassman, *Arms for the Arabs* (Baltimore, 1975), pp. 85-86,
38. Sadat (*note* 24), p. 198 ; Heikal (*note* 24), pp. 140 ff.
39. Rubenstein (*note* 31), pp. 121-122.
40. *Soviet News*, 1 September 1970, pp. 73-74.
41. *Soviet News*, 13 October 1970, pp. 13, 19.
42. Whetten (*note* 15), p. 122. See also Sadat (*note* 24), pp. 276-280.
43. *Ibid.*, p. 151.
44. Sadat (*note* 24), pp. 221-222 ; 279-282.
45. Heikal (*note* 24), p. 146.
46. *New Times* (19), May 1971.

CHAPTER VI

The War of 1973 and After

Background

The period from June 1967 to the death of President Nasser on 26 September 1970 was marked by a pattern of progressively increasing Soviet involvement in the Arab-Israeli conflict. In order to redress the regional balance which had been seriously disturbed by American supply of strategic aircraft and sophisticated weaponry to Israel, and to offset the threat posed to the survival of pro-Soviet progressive regimes, the Soviet Union decided to intervene physically by inducting into Egypt its latest air defence system and an estimated 20,000 personnel to handle it. At the same time, to reduce the cost of the Soviet commitment in Egypt and to avoid the risk of escalation and superpower confrontation, the Soviets supported Rogers' Plan II which defused the situation. But when the Jarring mission and four-power talks failed to deliver peace the Soviet Union fell back on a strategy of creating a durable stalemate on the Suez Canal front by erecting, towards the spring of

1971, a formidable system of air defence of the entire Nile Valley and the west bank of the Canal, thereby making Israeli aggression against Egypt almost impossible. The change of regime in Egypt did not bring any uncertainty or change in Soviet policy at least during the first few months. However, strains in Soviet-Egyptian relations were generated soon by a host of developments that were taking place ever since the enforcement of the American-sponsored ceasefire on 7 August 1970. Among these were : divisions and confusion among Arab ranks due to the Rogers' peace plan ; Soviet inaction during the Jordanian crisis of September 1970 ; receding prospects of a political settlement ; rising unrest and domestic pressure in Egypt for action to regain the lost territory ; growing anxiety over the freezing of the status quo due to the expanding detente between the superpowers ; concern over the rising burden of the Soviet aid on Egypt ; resentment against the Soviet Union for its veto on the Egyptian war option and restrictions on the supply of arm ; Sadat's disappointment over his failure to force Israeli withdrawal through American pressure ; his elimination of the pro-Soviet power-base in Egypt during May 1971 ; and finally, Sadat's disenchantment with the Soviet-Egyptian treaty which he had accepted in the hope of receiving arms in sufficient quantity to prepare for the war.

The hopes based on resumption of the Jarring mission in January and extension of the ceasefire in February for one month were belied. The ceasefire was not extended after 7 March and in the face of Israeli obstructionism Jarring suspended his mission indefinitely in April. On 19 September the UN Secretary-General in his annual report to the General Assembly testified that there was "little useful purpose" in reactivating the peace talks so long as Israel failed to commit itself to a withdrawal from the occupied areas. The year ended with the ritual passage of a resolution sponsored by 22 non-aligned states on 21 December calling for Israeli withdrawal from the occupied areas and implementation of Resolution 242. The Egyptians soon realized that their dependence on the Soviet Union had ensured protection from Israeli raids but not liberation of the occupied areas. Some Egyptians began advocating normalization of relations with the USA with a view to inducing Israeli withdrawal with the American pressure. Heikal, for instance, was of the opinion that Egypt was at war with Israel not with the USA. He advocated a pragmatic rethinking of relations with Washington.[1] However, the resumption of the American initiative was overtaken by the signing of the Soviet-Egyptian treaty. Later on, when reports of American agreement to sale of arms to Israel in excess of her legitimate defence needs of granting of licenses to her for the manufacture of sophisticated arms and aircraft domestically became known, the Egyptian leadership seemed to have become desperate over the prospect of a permanent freezing of the status quo.[2] It is almost certain that President Podgorny during his January 1971 visit to Cairo did not make a declaration that the USSR would support a resumption of the war of attrition.[3] To pacify the domestic public, Sadat had declared to make 1971 "a year of decision." (A group of prominent Lebanese politicians visiting Moscow in September 1971 was told that the Soviets would help the Arabs, but would not fight in their place.)[4] With this aim in view he again visited Moscow from 11 to 13 October 1971[5] to press his request for "decisive" weapons for a war against Israel. He was promised deliveries of requested arms towards the end of the year. When they did not materialize, Sadat reportedly sought on 12 December a meeting with the Soviet leaders. The Soviets replied towards the end of December by proposing that he could visit Moscow on 1-2 February 1972, a month after the passage of his "year of decision."

On 2 February 1972 Sadat paid a visit to Moscow at his own initiative. A lukewarm joint communique issued after the meeting repeated the standard denunciation of Israeli aggression, called for implementation of Resolution 242 and assured Egypt of Soviet assistance in strengthening its defence capacity.[6] Observers have attached great importance to this meeting as a decisive event in the development of Soviet-Egyptian rift. Sadat is said to have gone to Moscow with an "either-or" presentation. Either offensive arms are given by Moseow or Egypt will embark on a policy of arms self-sufficiency and reduction of external constraints on its policy options.[7] Sadat visited Moscow again from 27 to 29 April.

This time, the joint communique after a denunciation of Israel and promise of further strengthening of mutual cooperation between the two sides, added that "The events of recent months clearly show that the circles hostile to progress in the Arab East and their agents have not given up their plans for breaking the will of the Arab peoples, frustrating a political settlement, and making them succumb to the demands of the imperialists. In these conditions, the Arab states against whom aggression has been committed have every justification for using *other means* as well to regain the Arab territories captured by Israeli."[8] (emphasis added).

This was merely a sop, since Sadat failed to secure arms that would enable Egypt to "eliminate the consequences of Israeli aggression" as provided under Article 8 of the Soviet-Egyptian Treaty of Friendship and Cooperation. The "other means" were no more available in 1972 than they were in 1971. This stipulation was again repeated in the communique issued after the visit of Egyptian Prime Minister Aziz Sidki to Moscow on 13-14 July.[9] It represented the Soviet side's only concession whieh was so innocuous. Meanwhile, the Egyptian public and leadership were seriously disenchanted with the mounting cost of Soviet arms and services. Total financial indebtedness to the Soviet Union by then had reached nearly £ 5 billion and was increasing at the rate of £ 5 million per day.[10] The Soviet-American summit conference held in Moscow in May 1972 had done nothing to break the stalemate of "no war, no peace." It was against this background that Egypt expelled the Soviet military advisers on 16 July.

The reason why Soviet policy in the Arab East became immobilized at this time may be found partly in the detentist orientation of Soviet foreign policy in pursuance of the decisions of 24th Congress of the Communist Party of the Soviet Union held in March 1971. Moscow's quest for security in Europe, its need for advanced technology and credits from the West, its participation in the talks for SALT, its treaty with Federal Germany, the twin conventions formulated with American cooperation in March and April 1972 prohibiting chemical and biological weapons on the seabed and finalized in May, and many other steps were manifestations of the spirit of understanding and cooperaton between the two superpowers. The pursuit of detente at the bilateral level was hardly compatible with the pursuit of a forward policy in the Arab East. Hence Soviet commitment to the elimination of the hotbeds of war in the area, rather than sponsoring a war which would jeopardize their nascent detente with the USA. Heikal had a realistic and balanced view of Soviet policy in mid-1972 when he wrote : "The Middle East crisis is a crisis of our life in this area, but to the Soviet Union it is one of several crises in the world. Consequently, the Soviet Union can tolerate the state of 'no peace, no war' in the area better than we can. All this does not mean that the Soviet Union wants this state to continue. It definitely wants it to end, an end which will not involve it with the United States in any circumstances, a peaceful end if possible. As for the alternative, the Sovieit Union does not prevent any one from pursuing it nor does it push any one towards it."[11]

In conclusion, Soviet limitation on the supply of arms to Egypt from late 1971 till 1972 appears to be motivated not by any Machiavellian desire for keeping the Arabs dependent on the Soviet Union but by the genuine Soviet self-interest in a changing international situation.

The Soviet-Egyptian Treaty of Friendship and Cooperation, signed on 28 May 1971, was widely seen not as an act of colonization or satellization of Egypt, but as *an act of calculated control of the preservative nature.* It was begotten by certain developments in Egyptian domestic and foreign policy which were seen as detrimental to the Soviet interest.

Such radical steps by Sadat, within six months of his assuming office, as his insistence on a war of liberation against the Soviet counsel ; his collaboration with the plan for a federation of three Arab countries opposed by the Soviets ; his dismissal of Ali Sabry, regarded to be Moscow's man, and liquidation of his followers ; his discreet contacts with President Nixon and Secretary of State, Rogers ; and finally, his uneasy relationship with the Soviet leaders and his unpredictability—made the Soviets apprehensive about the future of their influence in Egypt. To test his fidelity and reliability they offered *him a choice* between a 15-year treaty of friendship institutionalizing Soviet-Egyptian relations and requiring Egypt to consult with the Soviets on major issues or termination of Soviet-Egyptian cooperation. In return to Egypt's fidelity the Soviet Union undertook to provide military assistance to Egypt to liquidate the consequences of Israeli aggression. In return to Soviet aid, Egypt promised to consult with the Soviets on all matters of common interest. This was the essence of the treaty. The Soviets wanted a measure of control over Egyptian decision-making so that nothing was done which was subversive of its position in Egypt or its relationship with the USA. In compliance with the Soviet wish, Egypt gave up its friendly approaches to the USA and abandoned the pursuit of an interim accord resulting in the reopening of the Suez Canal. The communique issued after the exchange of instruments of ratification of the treaty contained this stipulation : "... it was noted that the matter of opening the Suez Canal to international shipping could not be decided in detachment from other aspects of settlement and had necessarily to be tied up with agreement to have all Israeli troops withdrawn to behind the line existing before 5 June 1967 coupled with a firm deadline for this withdrawal."[12]

The treaty's ineffectivity in arresting the erosion of Soviet influence in Egypt became manifest on 7 July 1972 when Sadat, in retaliation to the low-key policy of the Soviets and without prior consultation with them, peremptorily terminated the services of the Soviet military advisers.[13] Its military significance was lost as soon after the October 1973 War as Egypt decided to negotiate a territorial settlement with Israel under the American auspices. It was unilaterally abroagated by Egypt on 14 March 1976 and naval facilities given to the Soviet fleet under previous agreements were terminated.

In retrospect, it appears that Sadat had reached the conclusion that, in view of Soviet opposition to a war against Israel and its restraint on the supply of arms, Soviet presence had become more a liability than an asset. It tended to perpetuate the stalemate of 'no war, no peace". It acted as a severe constraint on Egypt's freedom of manoeuvre in diplomacy and war. But Sadat was in a serious military-political dilemma : A political settlement with Israel was possible only under American auspices ; but normalization of relations with America was ruled out by Soviet presence on the Egyptian soil. By the same token a war could not be waged without the assistance of the Soviet Union which was, as a matter of principle, opposed to it and put a *de facto* embargo on the supply of offensive weapons. Sadat decided to terminate the Soviet military presence which saved Egypt the enormous cost of Soviet assistance and restored to it the freedom of action. Sadat at the time gave three reasons for his action : Sovit unwillingness to provide offensive weapons ; its failure to deliver weapons in quantities and on the dates promised ; and its excessive caution as an ally on the use of weapons already given.[14] Two more reasons given by him after the war of 1973 were : It was essential that the Arabs and not the Soviet Union got the credit for the decision to go to the war, and expulsion of Soviet presence was necessary to have freedom of deciding the time and manner of an attack.[15]

The Soviet response to the Egyptian action was determined by the calculus of cost and benefit. It quickly decided to withdraw its forces from Egypt and tried to reinforce its presence further north in Syria and Iraq as substitutes of Egypt. A Tass statement issued on 20 July gave this stoical explanation of the Soviet withdrawal : "The Soviet military personnel has fulfilled its functions in the Arab Republic of Egypt. Taking this into consideration and after an exchange of views between the two countries ; it has been considered expedient to return to the Soviet Union the military personnel which had been sent to Egypt for a limited period. This personnel will be withdrawn in the near future."[16] Various motives which have been adduced for the Soviet decision to withdraw from Egypt include (i) Soviet disappointment over the anti-Soviet actions of Sadat and growth of anti-Sovietism in Egypt and Sudan (ii) doubts over the possibility of Egypt's transition to Soviet-style socialism and its becoming a dependable ally ; (iii) a reappraisal of the Soviet-Arab policy in light of improving relations with the West and weighing of benefits accruing from detente over the cost of regional commitments ; (iv) dispensability of Egypt in view of the success of Soviet Mediterranean strategy resulting in relative strategic mobility and independent capability to back diplomacy by military power ; and (v) availability of other centres of influence in the area.

That the last factor might have been prominent in Soviet thought is borne by later developments. The joint communipue issued after the talks between Saddam Hussain, Vice-President of Iraq, and the Soviet leaders in Moscow on 17 February 1972 decisively "condemned the attempts of international imperialism to spread anti-communism and anti-Sovietism in order to interfere with the solidarity and cooperation of Arab countries and peoples with their faithful friends—the Socialist States."[17] On 9 April Soviet Premier Kosygin arrived in Baghdad to sign a 15-year treaty of friendship and cooperation with Iraq largely on the model of the Soviet-Egyptian treaty.[18] Arms supplies to Iraq were stepped up. The Soviets encouraged Iraq to nationalize the Iraqi Petroleum Company and extended aid for the development of new oil fields. Supply of arms to and training of military personnel in Syria were stepped up and Syria was also pressed for concluding a friendship treaty which it did not sign till 1980. All this signified that the Soviet Union as a great power had no intention of isolating itself from the area altogether. Rather, throughout 1972-1973 it continued to consolidate its position in the Arab East.

Towards the Arab-Israeli conflict the Soviet Union strictly maintained the same moralistic position which it had formulated after November 1967, namely, seeking a political settlement within the framework of Resolution 242. The continuity of this position was emphasized in an *Izvestia* editorial on 25 September : "Soviet policy with regard to the efforts of the Arab peoples to erase the consequences of Israeli aggression was and remains clear-cut, principled and consistent. Our country in all firmness states that it is necessary to abide by all the provisions contained in the well-known Resolution of 22 November 1967, and above all, the main one to the effect that the Israeli troops should withdraw from all the occupied Arab lands and that the legitimate rights of the Arab people of Palestine be guaranteed."[19] But removal of the "hotbed of war" from the region assumed top priority in the interest of preservation and promotion of detente.[20] During the summer of 1973 the Soviets launched yet another diplomatic offensive in favour of a political settlement. Perhaps the reason for this oft-repeated emphasis on this formula was the Soviet desire to distract Sadat from the war path.

At the San Clement Summit of June 1973 between President Nixon and Soviet Communist Party General Secretary Brezhnev the Soviet policy remained one of combining normalization of relations and detente with the USA with a search for a "just" (i.e., pro-Soviet) settlement of the Arab-Israeli conflict. Nixon has recorded in his memoirs that "Brezhnev tried to reach an informal agreement on principles of a Middle East settlement favourable to Arabs....Brezhnev was aware of the slow but steady progress we had been making in reopening the lines of communication between Washington and the Arab capitals and he was also aware that if America was able to contribute toward a peaceful settlement of Arab-Israeli difference, we would be striking a serious blow to the Soviet presence and prestige in the Middle East."[21] But as claimed by Primakov, it was on the "insistence" of the Soviet Union that the United States agreed to include the statement on recognition of the Palestinian people's legitimate rights in the text of the joint communiquer.[22] However, the Soviets seemed to be concerned more with securing recognition of their own right as a regional power in West Asia than of the rights of the Palestinians.

After a pause of estrangement from the Soviet Union Egypt, having failed to tap alternative sources of arms, decided to renew military relations with the Soviet Union. When Egyptian Prime Minister Aziz Sidki visited Moscow from 16 to 18 October relations seemed to have improved. The anti-Soviet General Muhammed Sadia had been dismissed to assuage Soviet feelings.[23] Extricated from the "hotbed of war" the Soviets now saw no risk in playing the role of a neutral merchant of arms. Arms began to flow once again. In joint communiques, the Soviets continued to recognize the right of the Arabs to use "other means" for liberation of their lands, a formulation first used in April.[24]

The new military relationship seemed to be based on the assumption that Egypt ought to be free to launch a limited, not general war, without Soviet control or supervision. It was not until February 1973 that the two parties found a satisfactory working relationship following the two visits to Moscow by Sadat's national security adviser, Hafiz Ismail from 7 to 10 February and by the new war minister, Ahmed Ismali Ali from 26 February to 2 March.[25] The Soviets were now apparently willing to meet most of the Egyptian requests for arms. In April Sadat admitted that the Soviets were doing their best given their continuing commitment to a peaceful political settlement.[26] Nevertheless, Sadat in his May Day speech reminded the Soviets that the continuation of the ceasefire was an American policy and the American talk of a peaceful solution was a "deception".[27]

The dilemma of Soviet policy at this juncture was how to reconcile the Soviet national interest with Egyptian national interest. It found a way of resolving this dilemma by a policy of temporization (i.e. delaying for the sake of delay). According to Kissinger, the Soviets opposed a partial accord on the Suez Canal as it would enhance American influence in Egypt and for the same reason they opposed a separate Egyptian-Israeli settlement. They recognized Egypt's right to launch a limited offensive but opposed a general war as in their view it would result in Arab defeat and jeopardise detente. Kissinger testifies that in their talks with the Americans the Soviets were pessimistic about Arab performance. The Soviets saw in this "half policy" of acquiescing in a "limited" but not an "all-out" attack the safest means of procrastination.[28] From February 1973 till the outbreak of the war, the Soviets on the one hand supplied the weapons to assist in the Arab war effort but on the other hand opposed the war both publicly and privately and urged a political settlement.

Soviet Role during the October 1973 War

So far as the genesis of the October 1973 war is concerned, it may safely be assumed that the decision this time, as during the crisis of 1967, rested with the regional actors. Just as Nasser's decision to go to the brink was based on his perception of the Egyption national interest, so was Sadat's to prepare for a war because a passive line was likely to result in his deposition, annexation of the Egyptian territory by Israel and loss of Egypt's prestige in the Arab world. Hafiz Ismail's mission in February 1973 to London, Paris, Bonn, Moscow, Washington and New York in search for a diplomatic breakthrough had failed. The search for alternative sources of arms had been futile. Sadat had to fall back on the Soviet Union for arms and on the oil-rich Arab states for money to execute his war plan.

The Soviets, anxious to halt further erosion of their influence in Egypt, agreed to a limited offensive across the Suez Canal and provided latest arms and equipment in sufficient quantities to ensure that the Arabs were equal to the Israeli on the battlefield. Yet the Soviets were not made a party to the Arab war plan. Although they were aware of Arab intention and even received informal information about the impending attack early in October, it was not a request for Soviet permission but a *fait accompli*.[29] As Quandt has observed. "If instead of being active partners in planning a campaign against Israel, the Russians remained sceptical of the outcome of such a venture, one might expect a somewhat more ambiguous policy. On the one hand, arms would continue to be delivered, perhaps even on an accelerated schedule, to ensure against subsequent charges that the Russians had engineered the Arabs' defeat by withholding vital supplies, but the Russians would not wish to be more visibly associated with what must have seemed a risky enterprise. If the Arabs were determined to act, Moscow would not try to prevent them, nor would it publicly reveal their intentions. At the same time, the Russians seem to have wanted to be in a position to avoid being drawn into the war against their will. Above all, the war must appear to be the primary responsibility of Egypt and Syria.[30] Kissinger has testified that "No Arab leader whom I met immediately after the war gave credence to the charge of Soviet-Arab collusion. Sadat, Algerian President Boumedience, Syrian President Asad, whatever their differences, agreed that Moscow had been grudging in its support for the Arab cause, slow in its delivery of arms, and eager to press for a ceasefire from the first day of the war."[31]

Once the war broke out on 6 October, Soviet objectives seemed to be threefold : (1) to prevent the war from precipitating a direct Soviet-American confrontation ; (2) to limit the effects of the war upon detente ; and (3) to regain and promote Soviet interests in the Arab world. A fourth objective which was shared by the USA was that their sponsored states "should not be subjected to defeat and humiliation. Both the great powers saw a military stalemate as the most realistic approach to a durable political settlement."[32] In pursuit of theses objectives the Soviet Union sought a ceasefire from the very first day of the war ; maintained close contacts and sought coordinated action with the USA ; and despite the massive American airlift of arms to Israel, Soviet propaganda did not seriously implicate the USA and depicted the war as an Arab struggle. On the other hand, in pursuit of its regional interests the Soviet Union exhorted the Arab states to render all possible assistance to Egypt and Syria ; encouraged them to put an embargo on oil supplies to pro-Israeli Western states ; undertook early in the war a massive airlift of arms ; and finally threatened unilateral intervention when Israelis penetrated the west bank of the Suez Canal in violation of the UN-sponsored ceasefire of 22 October 1973.

The initial Soviet reaction to the Arab attack was one of reserve. Within six hours of the outbreak of hostilities, according to Heikal, Soviet Ambassador V.A. Vinogradov called on Sadat to inform that the Syrians were prepared to accept an early ceasefire and that this policy had the Soviet approval. Sadat himself verified this only to find that the Soviets were misleading him. When Vinogradov came to Sadat the next day with the same request Sadat is reported to have told him that he was misinformed about Syrian intentions.[33] During 7-8 October the Soviets were busy in soliciting American support for a ceasefire and maintained a posture of non-involvement. The Soviets repeated to the Egyptians their call for a ceasefire daily for several days until Sadat finally ended it by insisting on continuing the war until he had shattered the myth of Israel's invincibility. This is corroborated by Kissinger's account : "Sadat's account—unlikely to be coloured by sympathy for the Soviet leadership—coincides with what the Soviets were telling us over the same period. Shortly after 8 : 00 A.M. on Wednesday, October 10, Dobrynin called on me with a message he declared important : the Soviet consultation with Egypt and Syria had been 'protracted' and 'not easy'. Nevertheless, Moscow could now tell Nixon that the USSR is ready, not to block adoption of a ceasefire resolution in the Security Council.' In other words, the Soviet Union would abstain from a resolution favouring a simple ceasefire in place ; it would veto a call for a return to the pre-war lines. In addition, the Soviet note expressed willingness to work for a negotiated settlement 'on the basis of liberation of all Arab lanes occupied by Israel."[34] (It is altogether a different matter that the United States accepted the Soviet proposal for ceasefire in place "in principle" to inhibit a Soviet diplomatic offensive at the United Nations and to buy time at the battle-front, but delayed its implementation long enough to test the latest Israeli prediction of victory within forty-eight hours on the Syrian front.[35] Presumably, the rapidly deteriorating situation on the Syrian front had alarmed the Soviets. On 9 October Premier Kosygin sent a note to Algerian Presidene Boumedience to unite the Arab states behind Egypt and Syria. On the other hand, the Soviet Union took a critical decision on immediate airlifting of arms to Egypt and Syria. Golan suggests that Israeli bombing of Damascus that day seems to trigger the Soviet air and sealift of arms to the Arab states, which according to most accounts began on 10 October.[36] It marked the beginning of direct Soviet participation in the Arab war effort and was bound to invite counter-intervention by America in the form of airlift of arms to Israel. According to Quandt, Soviet behaviour during the war far form being governed by a pre-determined master plan was most plausibly bounded by several general principles, and within that framework, "it was primarily events of the ground that determined specific decision."[37] These general principles indicate the desire to retain their credibility as a superpower-patron by coming to the rescue of the sponsored states in impossible situations, and a determination to avoid a direct clash with the United States at all costs. Soviet concern for detente was practical and not governed by any academic considerations. They simultaneously pursued the goal of preservation of detente and the goal of preservation of the friendly regimes in the area. Thus, Soviet airlift may be seen as yet another example of a rescue operation similar to the one undertaken during 1970. This explanation is shared by Rubenstein who sees the Soviet airlift a essentially defensive in nature because of the centrality of Egypt in Soviet regional policy.[38]

Once started, Soviet airlift became sustained and grew in quantity. According to the *Strategic Survey, 1973* (London, 1974), some 934 round trips were flown altogether by Soviet heavy transport planes carrying a total of 15,000 tons. The material delivered by sea was not known. The US commenced its counter-airlift on 13 October and ammounced some £ 2.2 billion in military aid to Israel. Heikal says that "when the airlifts were finally halted it was found that the amount of arms which America had supplied to Israeli almost exactly balanced ton for ton, the amount which the Soviet Union had supplied to Egypt and Syria."[39]

Resolution 338

A turning point came in the war by 15 October when the Israelis succeeded in crossing the Great Bitter Lake and establishing a bridgehead on the west bank (the Deversoir bulge). Anticipating a possible turn of the war against Egypt, Kosygin arrived in Cairo on 16 October and held five meetings with Sadat till the morning of 19 October. Although authentic information about the Kosygin mission is not available, it became clear from later developments that Kosygin worked hard to persuade Sadat to accept a ceasefire.[40]

We learn from Kissinger that on 18 October, Soviet Ambassador Anatoli Dobrynin called on him with an urgent message from Brezhnev. Dobrynin is reported to have read him a three-part Soviet draft proposal for submission to the Security Council : (1) a call for ceasefire in place, (2) an appeal for immediate phased Israeli withdrawal within the shortest period of time, and (3) an appeal for "appropriate consultations" aimed at establishing a just peace. Kissinger says he told Dobrynin that point one of the Soviet proposal was acceptable but point two was not acceptable and point three required precision. He was deliberartely stalling on the talks, as he has admitted, in the expectation of better Israeli performance.[41] When Kosygin reached Moscow in the night of 19 October, Brezhnev sent a personal message to Washington inviting Kissinger for talks in Moscow. Kissinger arrived in the night of 20 October and immediately started negotiations for a ceasefire. Kissinger says that at their meeting on 21 October (when the tide of the war had definitely turned against the Arabs), Brezhnev reminded Kissinger that he had already accepted in principle the Soviet three-point plan presented by Dobrynin in Washington. "This was news to me since I had rejected two of the three Soviet terms. So I spelled out our position once again."[42] Bowing to the law of the situation, the Soviet leaders relented on their proposal. Avoiding to negotiate on the basis of a Soviet draft, Kissinger claims to have submitted a counter-proposal. Brezhnev and Kosygin readily accepted the Kissinger text but pressed for converting the stipulation for direct negotiations between the parties under appropriate auspices into a Soviet-American guarantee of the outcome—implying a condominium in the region. Kissinger rejected this idea. He instead defined "auspices" as the presence of the Soviet and American diplomats at the inauguration of the conference and thereafter only when basic issues were debated. "That too was accepted by Brezhnev and Gromyko with a minimum of haggling."[43] The result was the joint sponsoring of Resolution 338 which was unanimously adopted by the Security Council on 22 October 1973. It called for an immediate ceasefire in place, implementation of Resolution 242 and immediate negotiations between the parties concerned under appropriate auspices to ensure peace. Kosygin flew to Cairo and Kissinger to Tel Aviv to explain the great powers' position on the agreement. The same day Egypt and Israel accepted the ceasefire and Moscow proclaimed Resolution 338 a victory for detente and a major achievement of Soviet Union's "principled" policy.

Soviet sponsoring of Resolution 338 on the American terms signified a subtle shift in the Soviet diplomatic position on a settlement which has been described by Nixon in these words: "The terms of the ceasefire were especially notable because they were first in which the Soviets had agreed to a resolution that called for direct negotiations between the parties without any conditions or qualifications. It was also the first time that they had accepted a 'general call' for adherence to Resolution 242 and not insisted on Israeli withdrawal from the occupied territories as a prerequisite for any further negotiations."[44]

The Threat of Soviet Intervention

It has been noted that during the fighting of 6-15 October Israelis had succeeded in crossing the Great Bitter Lake and establishing their presence on the west bank. Subsequently, they kept pushing southward wiping whatever Arab resistance they met in the way. By the time the UN-sponsored ceasefire became operative, forward Israeli elements had cut the Cairo-Suez City road. Israelis also claimed to have destroyed over one-third of Egypt's fixed SAM sites west of the Canal. Israeli units were now firing on the Egyptian Third Army units east of the Canal from positions west of the Canal and south of the Little Bitter Lake. In the north they had cut the two roads connecting Ismailia with Cairo. When fighting was resumed on 23 October, Israelis, ignoring the second UN ceasefire call that day, pushed further south to Adabiya, a harbour on the Gulf of Suez, thereby completely encircling the Egyptian Third Army on the east bank and cutting its communications with the west bank. The Egyptian Third Army was composed of 20,000 men and over 2,000 tanks of two infantry divisions. There was no obstacle now in the way of an Israeli march towards Cairo.[45]

By the morning of 24 October Egypt was placed in an impossible situation. Israel with the American help had turned its defeat into a victory and was in a position to annihilate the Egyptian Third Army and march into Cairo. It was against this background that Sadat on 24 October appealed to the Canal zone to enforce the ceasefire. Sadat's appeal was publicly rejected by the White House on 25 October. Moscow was quick to grasp the turning-point in the crisis which forebode the collapse of the Egyptian army and regime and consequently the total loss of Soviet prestige in the area. The Soviets quickly decided to intervene more directly and drastically to rectify the situation. The question whether this time they looked farward to building merely a symbolic presence or more massive and powerful combat presence shall remain shrouded in mystery. According to American intelligence reports, Moscow diverted transport aircraft assigned to the seven airborne divisions that were deployed for the airlift of arms to Egypt and Syria back to the assembly points, in preparation for a possible movement of Soviet forces into Egypt.[46] This is corroborated by Kissinger who has written that Nixon was led to believe by intelligence reports that "the Soviet Union was planning to send a very substantial force into the Mideast, a military force."[47]

Reacting to this situation, the Soviet Union first made a diplomatic move at the United Nations on 24 October when its representative Jacob Malik called for imposition of sanctions against Israel and then as the first hint of direct threat of intervention in the war declared : "I am fully authorized to declare that in light of the fact that Israel continues aggression, the proposal of Egypt to send contingents of the USSR and the US forces to the area of conflict is fully justified and in accordance with the UN Charter.[48]

When the USA rejected the Soviet suggestion for bilateral intervention in the conflict, Brezhnev sent an urgent message to Nixon, threatening of appropriate steps unilaterally to ameliorate the situation.[49] "There was a call from Dobrynin at 9.35 P.M.," records Kissinger, "It was 4.35 A.M. in Moscow but he had a letter from Brezhnev so urgent that he had to read it to me on the phone. I could see why. It was in effect an ultimatum : It proposed joint Soviet and American military forces to ensure the implementation not only of the ceasefire but also 'of our understanding with you on the guarantee of the implementation of the decisions of the Security Council'—in other words, the imposition of a comprehensive peace."[50] It was reminiscent of the Soviet note of 31 January 1970 declaring that if the United States did not stop Israel the Soviets would have to consider supply of arms to the Arabs to restore the balance. Reacting to the Soviet threat Nixon on the night of 24/25 October, put the American forces the world over on alert to meet an possible situation arising out of Soviet intervention. Nixon on 26 October admitted in a press conference that it was "the most difficult crisis we have had since the Cuban missile confrontation of 1962."[51] The

American alert seems to have been inspired by uncertainty created by the Soviet threat of intervention and was used by the USA to demonstrate to Israel that either it relax its stranglehold on the Egyptian Third Army or accept the necessity of Soviet airlift of supplies to it. Thus, despite the alert, the Soviet Union succeeded in compelling the United States to stop Israeli forces on the west bank and to save the Egyptian Third Army. Later, as a result of exchange of notes between Brezhnev and Nixon the situation was defused and the two gave joint support to Resolution 340 on 25 October which reaffirmed the ceasefire resolutions of 22 and 23 October and called for despatch of a UN emergency force to the Canal zone, excluding the troops from the five permanent members of the Security Council.

Brezhnev reciprocated the American cooperation on 25 October with an assurance of Soviet moderation. Speaking to the World Congress of Peace Forces in Moscow on 26 October, he dispelled all misgivings about Soviet intentions and moves in the recent crisis by saying that in response to President Sadat's request to both the Soviet Union and the United States to send "representative" (he meant observers) to the war zone to supervise the fulfilment of the UN ceasefire resolutions, the Soviet Union had already sent such representative. He emphasized that the Soviet Union was ready to cooperate in keeping the peace in the region and that "all the states and peoples of the area—I repeat, all of them—must be assured of peace, security and inviolability of their borders".[52]

An Assessment of the Soviet Role

Assessments of the Soviet role during the October 1973 War may be placed on two poles—on one pole is the harsh "conspiracy theory" of the cold-war warriors, which visualizes the Soviet behaviour before and during the war as a result of a well-conceived, intricate Soviet master plan for deception and expansion in the area. Like all unidimensional theories of Soviet foreign policy it also suffers from misconception and myopia and ignores the changing contours of international politics and superpower relationship. On the other pole is the mild "detentist" explanation of Soviet behaviour advanced by an Israeli scholar Galia Golan, according to which preservation of detente with the USA was the primary motivation of the Soviet policy and conduct during this crisis. Although detente was important, it did not mean abandonment of Soviet self-interest. Soviet policy remained concerned with both the preservation of detente and preservation of Soviet influence in the region. Hence, its ambivalent, uncertain, hesitant and incrementalist nature.

Detente was but one of Soviet interests. It could at times clash with other interests. Thus, all along, the Soviet leadership viewed detente practically, not dogmatically. After all, detente was an emerging working relationship between adversaries, not friends. It did entail some sacrificing of Soviet interests in the marginal areas. But the Soviets seemed to pursue their global and regional objectives concurrently, balancing one against the other. This dualistic approach was visible in all Soviet actions : Their airlift of arms to Egypt and Syria and within three days of the beginning of the war and Brezhnev's threat to intervene unilaterally to stop Israeli violations of the ceasefire and to save Egypt were at variance with detente. Yet despite the conflict of their interests they eventually cooperated with each other in managing the crisis by jointly sponsoring Resolutions 338, 339 and 340. Similarly, when contrary to the spirit of detente the Soviet Union was excluded from West Asian peace negotiations it did not result in Soviet withdrawal from the region at least to escape the detente uncontrolled client dilemma. Rather, it hardened its postures and aligned itself with the more intransigent elements of the "steadfastness front."

As Rubenstein has seen it, "Soviet policy in the crisis of October 1973 augured the advent of 'the new Cold War'—an evolving and competitive superpower relationship that seeks stability at the nuclear level, limited cooperation in areas of mutual concern, but continued rivalry at varying levels of intensity in pivotal regions of the Third World."[53] Kissinger has described Soviet diplomacy during the war as "clumsy, heavy-handed, unimaginative opportunism.... They were willing enough to fish in troubled waters but...loath to major risks ; their strength was not a master plan but the exploitation of the confusion of their adversary."[54] Cooperation with the United States which tended to undercut their presence or influence in the Arab world was disliked by them. Detente eventually collapsed by mid-1970 and by 1980 both the superpowers were engaged in a new arms race to negotiate from a position of strength.

Soviet intervention in the crisis of 1973 does not appear to be much different in intent, scope and effect from earlier Soviet interventions in the area in 1956, 1957, 1958, 1967 and 1970 which alike were defensive and preservative in nature. If Soviet intervention this time failed to secure or enhance Soviet influence in Egypt it is because its rival had made inroads into the Soviet beachhead. The Soviet Union lost its standing in Egypt when the latter realized that Soviet assistance could protect Egypt from Israeli aggression but could not make Israel give up Arab territory, while the United States had not only ensured an Israeli victory but was also in a position to force Israel to make concessions to the Arabs. After the war the Soviet Union was severely criticized by the Egyptians, Syrians and Iraqis for the dualism of its policy. Mutual discord between Cairo and Moscow reached to such an extent that Soviet arms supply was halted in 1974 and Sadat unilaterally abrogated the Soviet-Egyptian Treaty in 1976 and definitely turned towards the West. Syria too has pursued a policy of assertive independence since then despite her treaty of friendship with the USSR which it signed in 1980 under regional compulsions.

REFERENCES

1. *Al-Ahram*, 4 March 1971.
2. *Newsweek*, 31 July 1972. Anwar-el-Sadat, *In Search of Identity* (London, 1978), pp. 286-287.
3. *Keesing's Contemporary Archives*, 18, (1971-72), p. 24478.
4. *New York Times*, 17 September 1971.
5. *Pravda*, 14 October 1971.
6. *Pravda*, 5 February 1972. See also Sadat (*note* 2), pp. 227-228.
7. Lawrence L. Whetten, *The Canal War* (Cambridge, MSS. London, 1974), p. 210.

8. *Keesing's Contemporary Archives*, 18 (1971-72), p. 25279.
9. *Pravda*, 15 July 1972.
10. *Al-Ahram*, 31 March 1972.
11. *Ibid.*, 30 June 1972. Growth of Soviet interest in detente during the late 1960s and early 1970s was motivated by a variety of factors, domestic and foreign. The regime faced contradictory pressures of satisfying the military, yet needing to reduce defence spending to promote higer growth and greater satisfaction of the demands of the consumers. Detente afforded an opportunity for rational decision-making. It offered other eeonomic benefits, apart from the prospect of reduced and more efficient military budgets. Moreover, economic cooperation with the West held out the promise of toning up the economies of the Soviet bloc and dissolving incipient political unrest. See Valerie Bunce. "The Political Economy of the Brezhnev Era : The Rise and Fall of Corporatism". *British Journal of Political Science*, (2). April 1983 : 145-148.
12. *Pravda*, 5 July 1971.
13. Sadat later revealed that he announced his decision on the expulsion of the Soviet military advisers on 6 July in the presence of the Soviet Ambassador Vinogradov, who brought him a message from the Soviet leaders regarding the outcome of the Moscow summit and which made no reference to Egyptian requests for arms. The decision was executed between 7 and 16 July. Sadat (*note* 2), pp. 229-231.
14. *New York Times*, 25 July 1972.
15. George Lenczowski, "Egypt and the Soviet exodus". *Current History* 64 (377), January 1973 ; Lawrence L. Whetten, "Sadat's Strategic Options". *World Today* 29 (2), February 1973.
16. *Pravada*, 20 July 1972.
17. *Pravada*, 18 February 1972.
18. *Keesing's Contemporary Archives*, 18 (1971-72), p. 25201.
19. *Izvestia*, 25 September 1972.
20. E.g., Radio Moscow commentary, 19 June 1973, *SWB*/I, 21 June 1973 ; 28 June 1973.
21. Richard M. Nixon, *Memoirs* (New York, 1978), p. 285.
22. Y. Primakov, "The Fourth Arab-Israeli War". *World Marxist Reveiw* 16 (December 1973), p. 59.
23. *Keesing's Contemporary Archives*, 18 (1971-72), p. 25560
24. See *notes* 8 and 9 *supra*.
25. *Pravda*, 11 February 1973.
26. *Newsweek*, 9 April 1973; Sadat (*note* 2), p. 236.
27. Radio Cairo, 1 May 1973; *SWB*/IV, 3 May 1973.
28. Henry A. Kissinger, *Years of Upheaval* (New Delhi, 1982), pp. 209-210.
29. See Sadat (*note* 13), pp. 215-247; 287.
30. William B. Quandt, "Soviet Policy in the October Middle East War I". *International Affairs* (London) 53 (3), July 1977, p. 284.

31. Kissinger (*note* 28), pp. 469-470. According to Sadat, when he informed the Soviets about the coming war, they were so certain about Arab defeat that they evacuated the Soviet civilians from Egypt and Syria on 5 October. Sadat (note 13), pp. 246-247.
32. Whetten (*note* 7), pp. 286-287.
33. Sadat (*note* 2), pp. 252-263; Mohamed Heikal, *The Road to Ramadan* (London, 1975), pp. 212-215.
34. Kissinger (*note* 28), pp. 497-498; Sadat (*note* 2), pp. 252, 257-258, 259.
35. *Ibid.*
36. Galia Golan, *Yom Kippur and After* (Cambridge, 1977) p. 85.
37. William B. Quandt, "Soviet Policy in the October Middle East War II". *International Affairs* (London) 53 (4). October 1977.
38. Alvin Z. Rubenstein, *Red Star on the Nile* (Princeton 1977), pp. 235-236.
39. Heikal (*note* 33), p. 256.
40. *Ibid.*, pp. 245-246; Sadat (*note* 2), pp. 258-259.
41. Kissinger (*note* 21), 539-540.
42. *Ibid.* See also Nixon (*note* 21), p. 930.
43. Kissinger (*note* 28), p. 540.
44. Nixon (*note* 21), p. 936.
45. Sadat (*note* 2), pp. 261-262; 265-270; Whetten (*note* 7), p. 270.
46. *New York Times*, 25 October 1973.
47. Kissinger (*note* 28), p. 292.
48. *Ibid.*, p. 606 ; *Keesing's Contemporary Archives*, 19 (1973), p. 26200.
49. *Pravda*, 26 October 1973.
50. Kissinger (note 28), p. 606.
51. *Ibid.*, p. 583.
52. *Keesing's Contemporary Archives*, 19 (1973), p. 26201.
53. Rubenstein (*note* 38). pp. 277-278.
54. Kissinger (*note* 28) p. 1051.

CHAPTER VII

For Status Quo : Soviet Peace Moves Since 1948

A Survey of Early Attitudes

The Soviet attitude towards the Arab-Israeli conflict has been changing in response to the changing regional and international situations. The vicissitudes of Soviet policy may be traced through four distinct periods of Soviet involvement in this area : (1) 1947-1950 was the period during which the Soviet Union first asserted its interest to take part in deliberations over the affairs of this region. Its policy on partition of Palestine and role in consolidation of Israel by *de jure* recognition and arms aid was motivated by anti-colonialism and anti-feudalism. (2) 1950-1954 were the years when the Soviets were indifferent to the region and although leaning towards the Arabs they tried to maintain a stance of neutrality in the Arab-Israeli conflict. (3) 1955-1967 was the period of extension of the Cold War to the region. The main reason for Soviet rapprochement with the Arab East was the Baghdad Pact. To counter it the Soviets pursued a policy of anti-imperialism and polarization between the Arabs and Israelis. And (4) 1967-177 was a period during which the Soviets reappraised their attitude towards the Arab-Israeli conflict and were led to formulate a coherent and consistent policy towards the settlement of the conflict. Throughout these four periods the Arab-Israeli conflict has been subordinate to the strategic-political objectives of Soviet policy. The Soviets did not become involved in this regional conflict because of their internationalist duty to resolve it but because of its anti-imperialist potential and because it ensured Arabs' dependence on the support of the Soviet Union. In this section early Soviet attitudes will be summarized, then the context and motivations of the Soviet policy on a West Asian settlement will be explored.

(i) *Israel as a Nation-State* : At least in this respect the Soviet attitude has been consistent from the beginning to the end. As a great power, the Soviet Union is committed to the preservation of Israel as a nation-state. It was the first power to accord *de jure* recognition to Israel at its birth and sponsored its membership of the United Nations. Since then the Soviets never questioned Israel's right to exist as a nation-state. During the 1950s and 1960s they campaigned for the general, universal recognition of thc existing territorial boundaries of states and renunciation of force in resolving territorial disputes. Premier Kosygin, while inaugurating the emergency special session of the UN General Assembly in 1967, said that the Soviet Union *opposed aggressive activities of Israel against the Arab states but not its existence as a nation-state.* This point was repeated innumerable times and given added sanction through Resolutions 242 and 338.

(ii) *Direct Negotiations* : After the Armistice Agreements between Israel and her Arab neighbours, which were negotiated indirectly through the UN Conciliation Commission at Rhodes in 1949, the Western Power soon began advocating the need for direct negotiations between the Arab states and Israel to conclude a permanent peace and fix their boundaries. While Israel accepted direct negotiations on condition that Armistice boundaries were not altered and the Arab refugees were settled outside Israel, the Arab states rejected direct negotiations till Israel accepted the original partition boundaries and return of all refugees for resettlement in Israel. The Soviet Union identified itself with the Arab position till the passage of UN Security Council Resolution 338 in which it agreed to the principle of direct negotiations. In 1952 the Soviet Union had abstained from voting in the Ad Hoc Political Committee of the UN General Assembly on a draft resolution which called upon Israel and Arab states to enter into direct negotiations to resolve their differences, but defeated it in the General Assembly by voting against it.[1]

(iii) *Issue of Boundaries* : While the Armistice lines were initially regarded as temporary, the Western powers and Israel soon regarded them as permanent to be formalized through a peace treaty.[2] But the Arabs considered them as illegal as they incorporated about 6,000 square kilometres of the Arab territory seized by Israel in violation of the UN partition resolution. The Soviet stand till November 1967 had been in sympathy with the Arab stand. Soviet maps of Israel published during this period were careful to depict Israel's *de jure* boundaries as dual : (a) as the Soviet Union thought they should be in terms of the UN partition resolution of 1947 ; and (b) the *de facto* borders as stipulated in the Armistice Agreements of 1949. (A map of Israel published in *Izvestia* of 22 May 1967 followed the usual Soviet practice). After the passage of UN Security Council Resolution 242 the Soviets committed themselves to Israel's borders as they existed on 4 June 1967.

(iv) *The Problem of Refugees* : When the UN General Assembly passed its famous Resolution 194 (III) on 11 December 1948 the USSR's sympathies were still with Israel. The resolution provided that "The refugees wishing to return to their homes and live in peace with their neighbours should be permitted to do so at the earliest practicable date, and that compensation shold be paid for the property of those choosing not to return and for loss of or damage to property which, under principles of international law or in equity, should be made good by the Governments or authorities responsible."[3] The Soviet delegation opposed this resolution and voted against it. Soviet representative Andrei Vyshinsky was critical about the composition of the Conciliation Commission (only the Western bloc was represented in it) and about the failure of his draft resolution in the First Committee calling for the withdrawal of all foreign (meaning Arab) troops from Israel.[4]

Later, when the Soviet Union reoriented its policy towards the Arabs it began supporting the Arab case on the Palestinian refugees. Perhaps the first joint Soviet-Arab declaration upholding the "lawful rights of the Arabs of Palestine" was the one signed by Khrushchev and Nasser on 15 May 1958.[5] Thereafter, no Soviet-Arab joint Communique has ever skipped the mention of the "inalienable rights of the Palestinian refugees" in accordance with the UN General Assembly resolutions. Similarly, each year (since 1950) the General Assembly has discussed the report of the UN Relief and Works Agency (UNRWA) and approved its budget. Such occasions have invariably provided an opportunity for the expression of Soviet support to the Arab cause. When during the discussion in the Special Political Committee in 1959 the Israeli representative accused the Soviet Union of being inconsistent on the refugee problem, Soviet representative Arkady Sobolev replied tnat the Soviet delegation had voted against the Resolution not on account of its Paragraph 11, where the right was set forth, but on account of other provisions. Later, the Soviets continued to reaffirm the right of these refugees to repatriation and to compensation.[6]

Many more Arabs were displaced from their homes as a consequence of the June 1967 War. The Soviet Union in 1968 voted in the Special Political Committee in favour of a draft proposing effective and immediate steps for the return without delay of those inhabitants who had been displaced since the outbreak of war in 1967. In the opinion of the Soviet delegate speedy return of the new refugees would create more favourable political attitudes and help the mission of Gunnar Jarring.[7] He described as very important that part of the draft (Resolution 2535 (XXIV) of the General Assembly), which reaffirmed the "inalienable rights of the people of Palestine", raising them for the first time above the status of refugees.[8]

It is very interesting to know that the Soviet bloc adopted a negative attitude towards the UNRWA. The Soviet Union, Poland and Czechoslovakia abstained from voting on the draft in 1949 which created the Agency. With the exception of Yugoslavia, none of the countries of the Soviet bloc has ever contributed to the UNRWA, asserting that the problem of the refugees was a creation of western imperialism and Zionism and that those responsible for it should shoulder the burden of relief.

(v) *Jerusalem* : Although the UN resolution on partition of Palestine provided for internationalization of Jerusalem, divided as a a result of the Arab-Jewish war of 1948, between an Israeli sector and an Arab sector comprising the Old City which was later annexed by Jordan. Its status has since been in dispute. Soviet displeasure at Israel's close association with the Western bloc by 1949 was perhaps the reason of the Soviet delegation voting in favour of UN General Assembly Resolution 303 (iv) of 9 December 1949, calling for internationalization of Jerusalem. This gesture produced, no doubt, a favourable impression on the Arab block in the United Nations. However, the Soviets did not consistently observe the sanctity of the Arab position. If Eytan[9] is to be believed, on 17 April 1950, the Soviet Unton informed the Secretary-General that in view of the opposition of the people of Jerusalem it was withdrawing its support of the General Assembly Resolution on internationalization of Jerusalem. When in late 1953 the Israeli foreign ministry shifted its offices to Jerusalem, the envoy of the Soviet Union was among those first who presented their letters of credence to the Israeli chief of state in Jerusalem.

From then till 1967 the Soviet Union seemed to accept the status quo in Jerusalem. When as a result of the June 1967 war Israel captured the Old City and later took steps to integrate it with the western sector, the Soviet Union supported all UN resolutions calling upon Israel to rescind all measures to alter the legal status of the Old City of Jerusalem (General Assembly resolutions 2253 and 2254 and Security Council resolution 298 of 1971, etc.). Later, Israeli withdrawal from the Arab part of Jerusalem became an integral part of all Soviet plans for a political settlement in the area.

(vi) *Jordan River Waters* : Arab opposition to unilateral Israeli plans for the diversion of the waters of Jordan River revolved around its political and military aspects. The Arab League in 1955 rejected a Western-sponsored blueprint for a sharing of the Jordan waters on a regional basis. In sympathy with the Arabs Khrushchev during his May 1964 visit to Egypt openly supported the Arab case and condemned Israeli diversion of the Jordan waters.[10]

(vii) *The Suez Canal And the Gulf of Aqaba* : Soon after signing the Armistice Agreement with Israel, Egypt, exercising her legal rights as a belligerent, imposed a blockade against Israeli shipping through the Gulf of Aqaba and the Suez Canal till the resolution of the Palestinian problem. On an Israeli complaint the UN Security Council on 1 September 1951 called upon Egypt to lift the blockade. The Soviet Union abstained from voting on this resolution. When early in 1954 Israel turned again to the Security Council the Soviet Union vetoed a resolution which reiterated "grave concern" at Egypt's failure to comply with the Council's earlier resolution, and called upon Egypt "in accordance with its obligations under the Charter to comply therewith."[11]

However, in view of Arab sensitivity, the Soviet stand on the international character of the straits of Tiran and the Gulf of Aqaba remained ambiguous till 1967. Although the Soviet Union became a signatory to the 1958 Geneva Convention on the Territorial Sea and the Contiguous Zone (which the Arab states did not sign), it avoided to make any official comment on this issue till the adoption of Resolution 242. But in 1969 a Soviet commentator justified the Egyptian reimposition of the blockade of Aqaba on the ground that (i) this measure was necessitated by Israeli bombing of Damascus on 7 April 1967 and concentration of troops on the Syrian border ; and (ii) there were no special agreements on the Gulf of Aqaba and the Suez Canal linking them with the open sea. Egypt had acted under Article 14 of the 1958 Convention and at the same time agreed to hold talks on the status of the Gulf of Aqaba.[12]

(viii) *Emigration of Soviet Jews to Israel*: Russia was the first east European country which allowed its Jews to emigrate to Palestine after 1917. But till the 1960s the number of emigrants was negligible. During the 1960s the number of Jews permitted to emigrate from the Soviet Union averaged about 1000 annually (although the Soviets contradicted Western reports of mass Jewish emigration from the Soviet Union to Isracl).[13] With the onslaught of detente in 1971, however, this figure zoomed suddenly to nearly 14,000. It went on increasing. The year 1972 was called the year of the exodus of Soviet Jewry when about 56,000 Jews arrived in Israel mainly from Russia. In 1973, over 35,000 Jews emigrated to Israel. The process continued in 1974.[14]

Emigration of the Soviet Jews to Israel which strengthened the technological and military potential of Israel against the Arabs was bound to create misunderstanding in Arab minds. It became one of the reasons for Arab-Soviet discord during 1972. But Jewish emigration from the USSR was a matter of Soviet-American relations and a delicate part of detente at this point. The Soviet Union disregarded the susceptibilities of its Arab clients in the expectation of larger benefits accruing from detente.

Soviet Line on A Political Settlement Since 1967

Prior to 1967, the Arab-Israeli conflict had served well the Soviet purpose of pressing imperialism in its own backyard and supplanting it with Soviet presence whenever and wherever possible. That is why in its zeal for polarization of the Arab-Israeli conflict the Soviet Union never formulated a coherent, consistent and logical policy towards this conflict. However, the Arab defeat in 1967 had a number of disadvantages for the Soviets—it had lowered their prestige in the Arab world, it had created doubts about their credibility as a great-power patron, it had discredited one-billion-dollar worth Soviet-made arms and put their effectiveness in question, and last but not least, by destroying the regional balance of power had shaken the Soviet strategy in the eastern Mediterranean. But the Soviet decision to quickly restore the balance soon recovered their lost prestige. The Soviet Union committed itself to the defence of the pro-Soviet regimes but did not agree to underwrite a war of liberation against Israel as it now appeared to be putting a higher value on the thaw in its relations with the United States than on the emotional satisfaction of the vanquished.

Next, the USSR tried to restore to the Arabs what they had lost on the battlefield through international and great-power pressure but failed to repeat the performance of 1957. It lost the diplomatic battle for the condemnation of Israel for its June 1967 aggression and securing the withdrawal of Israeli forces from the occupied areas and was eventually forced to acquiesce in the Western-formulated vague principles of a settlement embodied in Resolution 242. The resolution soon became not a symbol of compromise and a basis of diplomatic give-and-take but a weapon of political warfare and diplomatic procrastination. Its generalities and ambiguities produced opposite interpretations as to its substance and the mechanics of its implementation. Nevertheless, the Soviet Union accepted it and made it the basis of its own peace diplomacy in the Arab world as well as in great-power and international forums. Accordingly, the Soviet Union formulated a coherent, consistent and ideological position on a political settlement centring on Israel's withdrawal from the occupied territories and restoration of the *status quo ante bellum.* This line fitted well with the current low-key Soviet regional and global policy.

The thesis of this chapter is that after 1967 the Soviets became genuinely interested in a political settlement and tried their best during 1968-1972 to procure a settlement on the Soviet-Arab terms. But this policy plank, if taken on its face value, would be seriously misleading unless one also takes into account its underlying political motivations, namely, Soviet desire to limit the scope of the regional conflict, to minimize the cost of Soviet commitments, and to prevent superpower collisions in regional disputes. This low-key policy of *temporization* in the Arab-Israeli conflict betrayed a conservative bias which represented a sharp contrast with the pre-1967 forward policy of *polarization*.

Why did the Soviet Union fortify its position around a

political settlement based on Resolution 242 despite its apparent thinness during 1968-1972 ? It seems that the Soviets were now weighing the cost of their involvement in the conflict against the benefits to be derived. *Second*, they might have wished to consolidate their gains in the client states and forestall unwelcome developments by obtaining a degree of control over the vulnerable decision-makers in these states. *Third*, they might have abhorred war because of its risky implications —loss of face for the Arabs and the USSR, mounting strain on a depressed Soviet economy from further aid and intervention, and greater risk of superpower confrontation. *Fourth*, they might have wished to perpetuate the present military and political dependence of the Arabs upon the Soviets. *Fifth*, they might have barred against the possibility of their commitment to the Arabs ending in "Vietnamization." And *finally*, Soviet policy of detente and cooperation with the USA might have inclined the Soviet leader to *de facto* compliance with the repeated American demand from the second half of 1971 till the end of 1972, for a Soviet arms embargo against the Arab states as any disturbance of the regional status quo was in their view likely to jeopardize the Soviet gains from detente. In a parallel move, the Americans, likewise interested in detente with the USSR, did not respond to Sadat's expulsion of the Soviet military advisers from Egypt in July 1972 and did not come out with a unilateral initiative for a settlement for fear of alienating or antagonizing the Soviets.

A brief survey of Soviet diplomatic moves during the period under review would illustrate the Soviet concern for a peaceful end of the crisis which was necessary to develop its cooperative relationship with the West as well as more pragmatic Soviet-Arab cooperation.

The Soviet diplomatic offensive for a peaceful settlement was opened early in 1968 with a major policy statement issued by the Soviet government which contained four key elements : (i) Israel was continuing its aggression of the last summer against the neighbouring Arab states and "expanding the scope of the crisis and its dangerous international consequences" ; (ii) Israeli home ministry had declared that the occupied Arab territories will not be considered enemy territory and accordingly Israel had been attempting to "turn the ceasefire line into its state border" ; (iii) UN Security Council Resolution 242 was not "a recommendation or an opinion that governments are free to take into consideration or disregard." Under the UN Charter, every decision of the United Nations is binding upon the Member-States ; and (iv) the Soviet Union was determined "to strive for the cessation of Israeli aggression and the liquidation of all its consequences, the return of the territories seized from the Arab states as a result of 1967 aggression to their legitimate owners and the realization of the necessary political settlement in the Near East on the basis of respect for the sovereignty, territorial integrity and political independence of every state in this area."[15]

This was followed up by Soviet Foreign Minister Gromyko's speech to the USSR Supreme Soviet on 27 June in which he declared : "We are taking every measure we can to do away with the consequences of the Israeli aggression, taking into account in the process the need to respect the sovereignty, territorial integrity and political independence of every state in this area, whether an Arab state or Israel."[16] He praised and supported the recent Egyptian proposal for a step-by-step withdrawal of Israeli forces. A *Pravda* leader on 3 December stated that "The Soviet Union is deeply concerned that despite all difficulties, the Middle Eastern crisis can and must be settled by political means. This is in the interest of all nations. The USSR...will not permit a new, dangerous flareup in the area." Gromyko then visited Cairo from 21 to 24 December to find a common ground with the Egyptian leaders for a Soviet initiative on the diplomatic front. The joint communique issued after the talks was significant for emphasizing two points : (i) The USSR government highly "appreciates" the position taken by Egypt and "notes" that she has announced its acceptance of the Security Council Resolution and its readiness to fulfil it, as well as to cooperate fully with the special representative of the UN Secretary-General Gunnar Jarring ; and (ii) the government of the UAR "highly appreciates" the steps taken by the Soviet government "for the liquidation of the consequences of Israeli aggression, the defence of the legitimate rights and independence of the Arab peoples and the establishment of a lasting and just peace in the area."[17]

The result was the first Soviet peace plan formally submitted in the form of a note to the United States, Britain and France on 30 December 1968. Published in *Pravda* in outline form on 25 January 1969, the plan called, *inter alia*, for acceptance of Resolution 242 by Israel and "those neighbouring Arab states willing to participate in the implementation of plan of action," proposed a time table and procedure for the phased withdrawal "under UN supervision" of Israeli forces from all territories occupied in 1967, and promised "secure and recognized boundaries," freedom of navigation in the region's international waterways" and "a just solution of the refugee problem." Agreed upon borders would then be guaranteed by the four big powers. Documents containing this agreement would be deposited with the UN on the day Israel commenced the withdrawal of its troops. This was a mere restatement of the principles of the Resolution 242 with the added features of a time table and a phased procedure for withdrawal of Israeli forces (both points first initiated by Egypt) and the four-power guarantee of the agreed-upon borders. The American reply to the Soviet note reflected the basic differences between the approaches of the two powers that existed from the days of the emergency special session of the UN General Assembly. Nevertheless, four-power talks within the frame-work of Resolution 242 were started in New York on the Soviet suggestion but were soon deadlocked. More definitive Soviet proposals were put on 17 June 1969,[18] in an article by Laptev in February 1970,[19] in an article by Belyaev in April 1970[20] and in an article by Primakov in October 1970[21] and in another article by him in January 1970.[22] All these statements contained these essential elements : (i) Scheduled, phased and UN-supervised withdrawal of Israeli forces and simultaneous termination of the state of war and establishment of peace between the belligerents ; (ii) withdrawal may be effected *after* a binding treaty signed by the parties concerned ; (iii) demilitarized zones may be set up on both sides of agreed borders and supervised by the United Nations ; (iv) a just solution of the refugee problem ; and (v) guarantee of the territorial settlement by the four big-powers. Moscow repeated its offer of joining the other powers in guaranteeing a settlement at the 24th Congress of the Communist Party of the Soviet Union held in March 1971.

Some diplomatic give-and-take did take place as a result of the four-power consultations. For instance, the first ever detailed American peace plan presented by Secretary of State William Rogers on October 1969[23] included some of the Soviet-Arab proposals such as a time-table for Israli withdrawal, a solution of the refugee problem and indirect negotiations to reach peace. It failed because the Soviets did not ultimately like an American-mediated peace and because Israel was too much afraid of American reapproachment with the Arabs. It could not believe in four-power guarantees and the UN peace-keeping force. The USA would not twist the arms of Israel whose strength and security was one of the cardinal principles of American West-Asia policy. The Soviet Union, moreover, was afraid of American "quite diplomacy" and any partial or separate peace settlements under American auspices which might erode the position of the USSR as a regional power. Israeli were not willing to accept anything less than a settlement dicated by them to the Arabs face-to-face. In these circumstances it was hardly surprising if the Soviet Union failed in its grand strategy of effecting an Israeli withdrawal from Arab areas through great-power pressures.

Soviet Preferences Since 1973

One contribution of the USSR to the post-1973 peace process was its agreement to the linking of the ceasefire of October 1973 with the holding of direct negotiations between the parties under appropriate auspices with a view to implementing Resolution 242 in all its parts. After the War the Soviets began to emphasize the following factors which were now conducive to a peaceful settlement : (a) the climate of detente in international relations ; (b) growth of cooperation between the two superpowers ; (c) destruction of the myth of Israel's invincibility and military superiority ; (d) Arab unity as demonstrated in the use of the oil weapon against the backers of Israel ; (e) Soviet support to the Arab cause, and

(f) Israel's isolation in the international community.[24] To the essential elements of pre-war peace plans were now added the participation of the Palestinians as an independent party in any negotiations for a settlement but the right of Israel to live within secure and recognized borders was also recognized. The dominant theme of Soviet diplomacy during this period was the pursuit of a settlement through an international peace conference including all the interested parties. The Geneva Conference which met for a brief inaugural session in December 1973 may thus be seen as a triumph for Soviet diplomacy.

The Soviet Union became suspicious of the American-mediated partial disengagement accords signed between Egypt and Israel in 1974 and 1975 and between Israel and Syria in 1974. It continued to assert that the reconvening of the Geneva Conference was necessary so that no one side could dictate its desired solution outside the Conference. In his report to the 25th Congress of the Communist party of the Soviet Union held in Moscow in February 1976, General Secretary Brezhnev stated : "As regards the Soviet Union, its position is a constructive and principled one. As the Co-Chairman of the Geneva Conference, the USSR is prepared to cooperate in all efforts to reach an effective settlement of the conflict. We are prepared to participate in international guarantee of the security and inviolability of the frontiers of all Middle East countries either in the UN framework or on some other basis. Incidentally, it is our opinion that Britain and France too could participate in such guarantees along with the USSR and the USA. This would only help matters. We are for creating conditions that would facilitate the development of our relations with all Middle East countries. We have no prejudices against any of them. Finally, we are also prepared to participate in a search for a solution to such a problem as ending the arms race in this region. But it stands to reason that this must be tied in closely with a general settlement in the Middle East. To take up the problem before such a settlement is reached would place the aggressor on a par with his victims."[25]

Tass on 1 October 1976 circulated a Soviet proposal for a comprehensive regional settlement (submitted to Egypt, Israel, the PLO, the USA, the UK, and France) based on the reconvening of the Geneva conference which should address itself to four basic issues : (i) complete Israeli withdrawal from all occupied areas ; (ii) termination of the state of war ; (iii) "ensuring the inalienable rights of the Palestinian people including their right to self-determination" and establishment of a Palestinain state ; and (iii) right of all nations including Israel to live in secure and recognized borders guaranteed by the greater powers.[26]

This position was further expanded in Brezhnev's speech at the 16th Congreess of the Trade Unions of the USSR held in Moscow on 21 March 1977 : "We consider, in particular, that the final document (or documents) on peace in the Middle East should be based on the principle that the acquisition of territory by means of war is impermissible, and on the right of all states in th: area to independent existence and sovereignty. It goes without saying that the inalienable rights of the Arab people of Palestine must be ensured, including their right to self-determination and establishment of their own state ... "[27]

The last joint Soviet-American statement which recognized the co-responsibility of the Soviet Union for making and maintaining peace in the area was issued on 1 October 1977. It declared that "the Soviet and American Sides believe that the only right and effective way for achieving a fundamental solution to all aspects of the Middle East problem in its entirety is negotiations within the framework of the Geneva Conference" which was to be convened "no later than December 1977.[28] However, Sadat by his sojourn to Jerusalem on 20 November 1977 had made a direct opening to Israel and the USA, thereby foreordaining the exclusion of the Soviet Union from the forthcoming Egyptian-Israeli negotiations. The Egyptian-Israeli Peace Treaty signed on 26 March 1979 in pursuance of the Camp David Agreements of the previous year was the greatest blow ever administered to the Soviet Union in this region. Even after exclusion from Egypt, Soviet commentators continued to reiterate Soviet preferences regarding a comprehensive peace-settlement in the area. Primakov, for instance, wrote in 1980 : "It will be impossible to attain a stable peace in the Middle East, if it is not a just peace. And a genuinely just peace can only be ensured on the basis of a tripartite formula : withdrawal of Israeli forces from all territories occupied in 1967, including the eastern part of Jerusalem ; granting of the right of self-determination of Palestinian people, leading to the creation of their state, if so desired ; and guaranteeing of security to all states and peoples inhabiting the region, including the state of Israel.[29]

Soviet Attitude Towards the Palestinian Movement

It is also interesting to isolate one aspect of the Arab-Israeli conflict, namely, the Palestinian national movement and to look into the vicissitudes of this attitude to illustrate the point of inconsistency in Soviet policy.

The Palestinians displaced from their homeland during 1947-1948, and again in 1967, ceased to be a "people" just as Palestine ceased to be a political entity after 1948. It was not until 1969 that UN General Assembly Resolution 2535 (XXIV) recognized the existence of those people and called for the restoration of "the inalienable rights of the Palestinian people." Soviet policy towards them, despite innumerable references to the legitimate rights of the Palestinian Arabs in Soviet-Arab joint communiques over the years remained ambivalent at best. It was not until 1974 when the Soviets anticipated the defection of Egypt from their camp, that they recognized the Palestine Liberation Organization (PLO) as the representative of the Palestinian people and allowed it to open its office in Moscow.

Although the Palestinian resistance movement came into being as early as in 1959 in the form of Al-Fatah and then consolidated with the formation of the PLO in 1964, it was hardly noticed by party and government circles in the USSR until 1967, when it was accorded support for the first time in a joint communique issued on 11 February after talks between CPSU functionaries and a visiting delegation of the Syrian Ba'th Party.[30] During the period 1967-1973, the Soviets followed a cautious policy towards the guerilla movement giving it moral and sometime material support (confined to the pro-Soviet factions). At the same time, the Soviets tended to regard the Palestinian resistance as unreliable and counterproductive. Soviet attitude towards it may be seen in light of post-Khrushchev shift in Soviet policy from universal support to radical-revolutionary and national liberation movements to a rather pragmatic cooperation with the established regimes in the third world areas. In the Arab East, first Egypt, then Syria became the lynchpins in the Soviet search for influence and allies. Given their firm rejection of extremism and adventurism in the wake of the 1967 War, it is inconceivable that the Soviets would have extended unqualified support to the guerilla aims and tactics. Thus, contrary to the guerilla aim of the liquidation of Israel, the USSR has consistenty upheld the right of Israel to exist within the Armistice borders. Just as they warned the Arab governments of the futility of warmongering, so they seemed to downgrade the importance of guerilla activity as a means of liberation and stressed political and diplomatic means.[31] The Soviet Union was opposed to violence and terrorism in the air irrespective of the political cause involved.[32] From 1967 to 1973 the corner-stone of Soviet policy towards the Palestinians had been the famous General Assembly Resolution 194 (III) of 1949 as reiterated in Security Council Resolution 242. In other words, the Soviets shared the Western view of the Palestinians as refugees and not as a people entitled to self-determination and political independence. When in 1974 it espoused the cause of Palestinian nationalism and called for the establishment of a Palestinian State on the liberated lands it was not out of moral persuasion but of political expediency.

During the Jordanian Civil War of September 1970 the Soviets kept their reserve and self-restraint and in the face of threatened American intervention on behalf of the Hashemite Kingdom, they pressed Syria to withdraw its tank divisions from Jordan where they had gone to save the Palestinian revolution from liquidation at the hands of the royalist forces.

The shift in Soviet policy in 1974 towards the PLO therefore, may be seen not in light of Soviet ideology but power politics. This change was motivated by regional factors as much as by the emerging superpower relationship. In recognizing the PLO as the sole representative of the Palestinian people the Soviet Union was in complete accord with the majority of the Arab states and the majority of the Member-States of the United Natinns. But what is significant is the Soviet demand that the Geneva Conference should provide PLO participation on a par with other parties. They now openly came out in support of the idea of a Palestinian State. From 1974 onwards the Soviet commentators and official spokesmen repeatedly raised the question of Palestinian self-determination and the necessity of a Palestinian State. Dimitriyev, for instance, wrote : "The political participation of the Arab people of Palestine in all the efforts to reach a just settlement in the Middle East must be supplemented with its geographical presence on the map of this region. The rights of the Arab people of Palestine must be observed to the full extent."[33] The aforementioned Tass statement of 1 October 1976 repeated this emphasis and this was followed the next year by a joint Soviet-American statement on West Asia issued on 1 October after talks between Soviet Foreign Minister Gromyko and US Secretary of State, Cyrus Vance, which included a reference to the "Resolution of the Palestinian question including securing the legitimate right of the Palestinian people." Later, Soviet commentator claimed that this reference to the Palestinian rights was included in the statement at the insistence of the Soviet sides.[34] However, the major concern of the Soviet leaders seemed to gain the American recognition of the legitimate right of the Soviet Union as a regional power.

The level of Soviet activity during the Lebanese crisis, arising out of Israeli invasion of Lebanon and the siege of Beirut in 1982, was lower than during any one of the previous regional crises. Indeed, the failure of the Soviet leaders to come actively to the aid of the beleagured Palestinians cast doubt on their desire and/or capability to influence the events in the region. However, heartened by Syria's resilience in the face of Israeli offensive, the Soviets punctuated their stance of "measured neglect" by circulating on 30 July 1984 an expanded version of their peace plan, which restated the well-known Soviet position on a regional settlement centring on the liberation of the Israeli occupied areas, establishment of an independent Palestinian state and international guarantees for the settlement provided by the Permanent Members of the UN Security Council.[35] As a means of facilitating that process it called for convening an international conference of the concerned parties to be cochaired by the USA and the USSR. The Plan evoked no response from the United States. Given the anti-Soviet postures of the Reagan Administration in its second term, the USSR is not likely to be accepted as a partner in the regional peace-making process.

This remained the diplomatic position of the USSR until the beginning of 1988 when she offered to resume diplomatic relations with Israel, provided the latter agreed to solve the Palestinian problem through an international conference.

The Advent of Gorbachev Era

Leadership transition in the USSR brought to prominence Mikhail Gorbachev as the General Secretary of the Communist Party of the Soviet Union, elected in March 1985. Throughout his three years in office, he has displayed an extraordinary drive in planning and implementing certain radical changes in Soviet domestic and foreign policy. Since the regime has come to stay it is pertinent to survey tentatively its major foreign policy initiatives and assess their possible implications for Soviet policy in West Asia.

A major contribution of the Gorbachev regime in the field of foreign affairs is what the Soviet scholars call a "new concept of foreign policy". The starting assumptions of this concept are the growing humanization of international relations and interdependence of the contemporary world ; the inter-*national* rather than class character of contemporary international relations ; the unfolding possibilities of the scientific-technological revolution for the progress of the mankind ; and the need for recognition of heterogeneity and diversity of the interests of the nation-states and for giving due consideration to them. In the light of these developments Gorbachev regime calls for realism and commonsense in foreign policy. It accords utmost importance to the common moral and humanitarian values of the mankind. It therefore aspires to break out of the mould of traditional policy of confrontation and defensive militarization or arms race with the West which only hinders the socio-economic development of the USSR and affects its international standing. It also calls for shedding old slogans and stereotypes. It prefers political to militaristic means of conflict resolution and upholds the path of negotiations, bargains and understandings to secure international peace and security. Hence a series of such initiatives as successive summit meetings between Soviet and Western leaders, broader contacts with the outside world, particularly the Third World countries, the Intermediate Nuclear Forces (INF) Treaty signed with the USA in 1987, and Geneva Agreement for withdrawal of the Soviet troops from Afghanistan in 1988, broadening of contacts between East and West Europe, and the general evidence of avoidance of entanglement in regional conflicts of the Third World.

The new political thinking subordinates foreign policy to the declared goals of domestic policy, viz., welfarism, economic restructuring, greater openness of the Soviet society, and political reforms and democratization. Foreign policy along with domestic policy is geared to the end of renewal of the Soviet society. By signing the agreements for partial nuclear disarmament Soviet leaders have claimed the credit for pushing back the danger of war.[36] They are certainly heading towards a deeper and more enduring detente with the Western world than achieved ever before.

Keeping in tune with these transformations at the global level, Soviet Third World policy is undergoing a subtle shift as well. Although they have not abandoned their commitment for the protection of pro-Soviet regimes, nevertheless, they appear to have given up their former ideological-partisan approach in favour of beneficial and pragmatic cooperation with regimes of all hues and colours. As a marked departure from the practice of the Brezhnev era, the New Party Programme, published in 1986, explicitly recommended cultivation of relations even with such Third World countries as follow the capitalist path of development. Sometimes, the Soviets have tried, as their recent overtures to Israel and Iran have shown, to maintain links with both sides of a regional conflict at the same time. One indication of the Soviet recognition of the economic potential of the Third world came from the report presented by Gorbachev on the 70th anniversary of the October Revolution when he specially mentioned such regional organizations of the Third World as the Organization of African Unity, the Arab League, ASEAN, SAARC, the Organization of the Islamic Conference (OIC), and the Non-Aligned Movement, calling attention to their great potentialities. In sum, Soviet Third World strategy is in transition, and as Hyland maintains, "Under Gorbachev the Soviet Union is likely to be more prudent in the risks and responsibilities it undertakes in the Third World. This reflects a new and more modest evaluation of the prospects for the Soviet Union. It also suggests that Gorbachev does not accept the proposition that the eontest with the West can be decided in the Third World. Indeed, he apparently believes the effort to gain a clear victory is too burdensome for the potential risks and gains."[37]

What are the implications of this metamorphosis in Soviet political thinking for Soviet policy in West Asia ? It is inconceivable that the Soviet Union, which deliberately tried to secure the status of a regional great-power over the past 30 years, could be permanently kept out of the peace process in the region. Evidently, the rigid status quo imposed by the Camp David Accords has not obliterated the need for peace and justice for all parties. Hence the Palestinian unrest and the so-called Shultz Plan. In fact, the Soviet Union was formally assigned a role in West Asia in the aftermath of the October War with agreements signed in pursuance of UN Security Council Resolution 338 which, by a later amendment, also called for convening an international peace conference in Geneva, with the USA and the USSR as co-chairmen. This conference had met for a procedural session for two or three days then adjourned sine die. Later, on 1 October 1977, a joint Soviet-American Statement on the principles of a settlement in West Asia was issued. It was scuttled by Egypt's unilateral peace with Israel. However, under the changed circumstances, this statement may again become the cornerstone of Soviet American cooperation for peace in this area. For, without Soviet participation there can be no durable peace there.

The dominant probability during the late 1980s is that the Gorbachev regime, with a view to appeasing and wooing the West for the success of its domestic programme, may tilt in favour of the Israeli-American position in the Arab-Israeli conflict, allow freer emigration of Soviet Jews to Israel, restore diplomatic relations with Israel, and, in an extreme eventuality, abandon the Arab cause altogether, though maintain state-to-state relations with individual Arab countries for mutual benefit.

One small indication of the things to come came in April 1988 when Gorbachev told the visiting PLO chief Yasser Arafat that "Recognition of the State of Israel and consideration of its security interests is a necessary element for the establishment of peace and good neighbourliness in the region based on the principles of international law."[38]

In sum, Soviet policy in West Asia has entered an era of transition. Its contours will be shaped in consonance with the eventual improvement in Soviet-American relations. It is nevertheless going to be inward-looking, down-to-earth pragmatic policy of seeking benefits wherever available. Moreover, Soviet interests are more likely to be cultivated, defended and promoted in the name of Soviet nation-state than the holy dogma of communism. In light of this trend such assertions that the recent Soviet overtures in West Asia "do not necessarily represent a shift in Soviet objectives or policy positions with regard to the conflict in the region"[39] or the statement that "a knowledge of Communist ideology is the key to understanding the nature and purposes of the Soviet threat and of how to respond to the Soviet Third World strategy"[40] appear to be misconceived as well as biased. They conceal the evolutionary nature of Soviet foreign policy.

REFERENCES

1. *GAOR*, 7th Session, 405th Mtg., 18 December 1952.
2. See Moshe Dayan, "Israel's Border Problems" *Foreign Affairs* 33 (2), January 1955.
3. Text in *GAOR*, I, 21 September—12 December 1948. *Resolutions*, pp. 21-25.

4. *GAOR*, III, 186th Plan., 11 December 1948, p. 990.
5. *Izvestia*, 16 May 1958; *Keesing's Contemporary Archives*, 11 (1957-58), p. 16228.
6. *GAOR*, 14th Session, SPC, 160th Mtg., 27 November 1959, p. 166.
7. *GAOR*, SPC, 633rd Mtg., 11 December 1968, p. 3.
8. *GAOR*, 24th Session, SPC, 686, Mtg., 5 December 1969. p. 240.
9. Walter Eytan, *The First Ten Years* (New York, 1958), p. 79.
10. *SWB*/I, 16 June 1960; *Keesing's Contemporary Archives*, 14 (1963-64), p. 20129.
11. Eytan (*note* 9), p. 94.
12. I. Blischchenko, "International Law and the Middle East Crisis". *International Affairs* (Moscow) (1), January 1969, p. 29.
13. *CDSP*. 11 (8), 25 March 1959.
14. *New Middle East* (41), February 1972, p. 3; Richard M. Nixon, *Memoirs* (New York 1978), p. 876.
15. *Pravda*, 23 March 1968.
16. *Soviet News*, 2 July 1968.
17. *New York Times*, 26 June 1969.
18. *New York Times*, 26 June 1969.
19. V. Laptev, "Middle East Divide". *New Times* (46), February 1970, pp. 4-6.
20. I. Belyaev, "Middle East Crisis and Washington's Manoeuvres". *International Affairs* (Moscow) (4), April 1970, pp. 30 ff.
21. *Pravda*, 15 October 1970; *New Middle East*, February 1971.
22. *Pravda*, 5 January 1972.
23. Unofficial text of the Rogers' proposals in *New York Times*, 22 December 1969.
24. E.g., G. Mirsky, "The Middle East". *New Times* (48), November, 1973, pp. 18-19.
25. Leonid Brezhnev, *Selected Speeches and Writings on Foreign Affairs* (Oxford, 1979), pp. 297-98.
26. *Arab Report and Record*, 1-15 October 1976, p. 617.
27. Brezhnev (note 25), pp. 299-303. See also O. Alov, "For a Settlement in the Middle East". *International Affairs* (Moscow) (9), September 1977.
28. *New York Times*, 2 October 1977; *Arab Report and Record* 1-31 October 1977, p. 881.
29. E. Primakov, "The USSR and the Developing Countries". *Journal of International Affairs*, 34 (2), 1980-81, p. 290.
30. *Asian Recorder*, 13 (1967), p. 7589.
31. E.g., I. Belyaev, "Ways of Ending the Middle East Crisis". *International Affairs* (Moscow) (10), October 1968, p. 28; M. Kruglov, "The Palestine Liberation Movement", *New Times* (37), September 1969, p. 13.
32. See *UN Monthly Chronicle*, 7 (11), December 1970, pp. 98-99; *Pravda*, 29 August 1972.

33. Y. Dimitrev, "Middle East: Need for a Just Settlement". *International Affairs* (Moscow) (10), October 1975, p. 750.
34. See note 28 *supra*.
35. *Pravda*, 30 July 1984.
36. Cf. 19th All-Union CPSU Conference (Moscow, June 28-July 1, 1988). "On Progress in Implementing the Decisions of the 27th CPSU Congress and the Tasks of Promoting Perestroika". Report by Mikhail Gorbachev, General Secretary of the CPSU (Moscow : Novosti, 1988).
37. William G. Hyland, "Reagan-Gorbachev III". *Foreign Affairs* 66 (1), Fall 1987, p. 9. For some recent writings on Soviet Third World policy see Daniel S. Papp, *Soviet Perceptions of the Developing World in the 1980s* : the Ideological Başis (Lexington, Mass. : Lexington Books, 1985) ; Jerry F. Hough, *The Struggle for the Third World* Soviet Debates and American Options (Washington, D.C. : Brookings, 1986) ; Francis Fukuyama, "Patterns of Soviet Third World Policy". *Problems of Communism* 36 (5), September-October 1987 ; and Stephan Sestanovich, "Gorbachev's Foreign Policy : A Diplomacy of Decline". *Problems of Communism* 37 (1) January-February 1988.
38. *Pravda*, 10 April 1988.
39. Galia Golan, "Gorbachev's Middle East Strategy". *Foreign Affairs* 66 (1), Fall 1987, p. 54.
40. Francis M. Casey, "The Theory and Practice of Soviet Third World Strategy". *Journal of Social, Political aud Economic Studies* 12 (2), Fall 1987, p. 258.

CHAPTER VIII

Conclusion

This study of Soviet foreign policy with special reference to the Arab-Israeli conflict addressed itself to a number of questions, namely, (i) How far is Marxism-Leninism relevant to the conduct of recent Soviet diplomacy ? (ii) Does it operate all the time from a preconceived blueprint or is it merely reactive to events ? (iii) Is it directed at the preservation of the status quo or at its revision ? The answers may now be summarized as follows :

The erosion of ideology as the main, even major determinant of Soviet foreign policy is by now an aceepted theme in the international relations literature. During the Khrushchevian and post-Khrushevian periods Marxism-Leninism has gradually receded as a guide to policy and action. Many of the hallowed doctrines of the past, including some basic theses of Lenin were abandoned or revised through the successive CPSU congresses held since 1956. Yet ideology persists as a language of analysis and as a methodology, and continues to serve a legitimatory function. However, erosion or de-radicalization of ideology is not the same thing as the end of ideology. Far from being redundant, Soviet ideology is a dynamic component of Soviet policy always adjusting itself to reality. There is still an irreducible minimum of Soviet ideology which orients the Soviet worldview, for instance, the basic belief in the ongoing conflict between forces of socialism and forces of imperialism, or the belief in the class nature of international relations.

That ideology is not the primary or even major motivator of Soviet policy in West Asia or the Arab-Israeli conflict is borne by the record of Soviet diplomacy in the area from 1947 to 1984. During 1945-46 the Soviet approach to the contiguous zones of the Balkans, Turkey and Iran was a recrudescence of the age-old Tsarist imperial policy of seeking strongholds or spheres of influence there. Successful local resistance and Western pressures forced the Soviets to desist from exerting pressure on these areas. But soon they found an opportunity to assert their interest in West Asia with reference to the Palestine question which came before the United Nations in 1947. Soviet policy on the partition of Palestine and support to Israel was hardly consistent with the consistent policy of anti-Zionism over the past thirty years. During 1955-1967, Soviet policy in the area cannot be understood except as a response to the challenge thrown by the West, first by the establishment of the Baghdad Pact and then by the stationing of the Polaris submarines in the Mediterranean directly threatening the Soviet industrial hinterland. These threats were offset by Soviet rapprochement with the bourgeois-nationalist regimes in the Arab East and by Soviet naval build-up in the eastern Mediterranean to offset the threat from the American Sixth Fleet. Thus Soviet policy cannot be considered apart from the global balance of power and the Cold war competition between the East and West at that time. Soviet advance in the region in a later period seems to be imperial in the classical, though not imperialist in the modern sense and was paobably as much involuntary as planned. During the 1960s, the forward Khurshchevian strategy of pressing imperialism whenever and wherever an opportunity arose, was replaced by a conservative strategy of "counter-imperialism" in the contiguous areas, that is, the desire for seeking influence by using such familiar imperialist methods as cultivating firm economic, political, cultural and military ties with the client states, concluding long-term treaties of friendship with them, and even seeking base facilities on their territory. Competition and self-restraint, expansion and coexistence have been the recurring patterns of Soviet conduct ever since the Bolshevik revolution. Far from aiming at world domination, Soviet behaviour, on the whole, appears to be "moderately, intermittently, and unexceptionally expansionist," rather than "relentessly, radically, and exceptionally expansionist."[1] Soviet behaviour, thus, does not appear to be much different from the behaviour of other traditional great-powers.

Despite the convergence-of-ideology-and-reality thesis, the Soviet leadership gives precedence to the concrete interests of the Soviet state (e.g., pursuit of expansionist goals) over ideological interests or proclivities which in a given situation do not coincide with or reinforce Soviet state interests. Hence, abandonment of the revolutionary or national liberation movements in favour of cooperation with the established regimes in the third world and subordination of the local Communist parties to the pro-Soviet bourgeois-nationalist regimes or insistence on their merger with the broad-based national coalition. Similarly, Soviet policy towards the Arab-Israeli conflict is hardly understandable without a reference to its underlying political motivations.

A definite purpose whether emanating from ideology or geography might have informed the Soviet conduct during an earlier period but in West Asia since 1950s it has not followed a uniform historical or ideological purpose constantly and relentlessly. In the Arab-Israeli conflict, particularly, Soviet actions have more often been reactive to events or responsive to opportunities than determined by a preconceived master plan. This is not to say that the Soviet Union did not have some interests or short-term objectives or preferences, or even some long-term objectives. Soviet diplomacy in the area over the petiod studied does not show the existence of any Soviet grand design for the area. Rather, it is reactive to events and receptive of opportunities.

During the 1950s, it became receptive to Arab nationalism and third-world non-alignment because of their inherent anti-imperialist potential. The Soviet-Egyptian and Soviet-Syrian arms deals were astute political moves to leap-frog over the iron-ring of the Northern Tier erected by the Western Powers. As soon as they got entry into the Arab East the Soviets began to expand their infiuence by such means as exploitation of the internal weaknesses of the Arab governments, inter-Arab tensions, Arab-Western and Arab-Israeli conflicts. The forward policy was put in shambles by the collapse of the Soviet-armed and Soviet-trained Arab armies during the June 1967 War. The Soviets thereafter adopted a low-key defensive policy till January 1970 when they reacted to the change in the regional balance of power effected by Israeli strategic strikes against Egypt. This time they intervened physically by assuming the responsibility of the aerial defence of the entire Nile Valley against Israeli strikes. It was essentially a rescue operation and not a move to sattelize Egypt as seen at that time. During the heyday of detente the Soviets were faced with the dilemma of balancing their developing relationship with the USA against their commitments to the client states in this region. They tried to overcome this dilemma by following an ambivalent policy to retain their gains in both the sectors. If on the one hand they sought to promote detente by such measures as allowing massive emigration of Soviet Jews to Israel, by imposing a *de facto* limitation on arms supply to the Arab states in deference to American wishes and committed themselves to prevention of a war in the region, on the other hand they actively assisted in the Egyptian war effort during early 1973 and once the war broke out undertook a massive air-and sealift of arm to the Arab armies and threatened to intervene physically when the Israeli forces established a stranglehold on the Egyptian Third Army by penetrating into the west bank of the Suez Canal by defying the UN ceasefire call of 22 October 1973.

Soviet policy towards the Arab-Israeli conflict during the period studied may be characterized as ambivalent, hesitant, incrementalist, shifting and compromising according to the perception by Soviet leaders of what constituted Soviet national interest amidst the existing correlation of regional and global forces. During the initial period, the Soviet rapprochement with the Arab East was not brought about by an intrinsic hostility towards Israel or filial loyalty to the Arabs. It was rather necessitiated by certain strategic-political considerations. Soviet policy towards the regional conatct was governed by these strategic-political considerations, rather than by any philanthropic or internationalist motives. Up to 1967, the Soviets never formulated a "policy" towards this conflict which they saw as a creation of Western imperialism which was better to be exploited to undermine imperialist positions. Nevertheless, they did take certain piecemeal stands on individual issues of the conflict to gain the support of the Arabs. In pursuance of their anti-imperialist strategy they polarized the regional forces ond thereby internationalized the Arab-Israeli conflict. If on the one hand they denounced the Tripartite Declaration of 1950, on the other hand they never openly challenged the legitimacy of the post-Armistice status quo and were rather committed to the general principle of the preservation of the existing state boundaries and pacific settlement of territorial disputes. Khrushchev, for instance, was reported to have told the Egyptians in 1964 that an Arab war against Israel would not solve any problem but may "trigger a third world war."[2] In a note sent by him on 31 December 1963 to all heads of states (including Israel and Arab states) he had given a universal call for renunciation of force in international relations and settlement of territorial disputes by peaceful means.[3] But Soviet Cold War diplomacy in West Asia not only made a negotiated settlement of the Arab-Israeli conflict almost impossible but objectively helped in bringing about thc crises of 1956 and 1967.

During 1967-1973, however, the Soviets came to realize the risks and pitfalls of their policy of regional polarization. The ensuing reorientation of Soviet policy was necessitated by the compulsion for balancing Soviet global commitments (e.g., preservation of international peace and security, avoidance of direct superpower confrontatlon, and promotion of detente and cooperation with the USA) against Soviet regional commitments (e.g., preservation of the pro-Soviet progressive regimes and cultivation of a regional sphere of influence). This reorientation was sought to be effected through (i) the formulation of an ideological line on a political settlement of the problem centring on thh UN Security Resoluion 242 of 22 November 1967, as a device for temporization at the regional level and diplomatic manoeuvring at the international level, (ii) a diplomatic offensive launched towards the end of 1968 to force Israeli withdrawal via international and great-power pressure, (iii) ensuring military parity of the Arabs with Israel and a durable stalemate between the two so that none was able to disturb the status quo ; and (iv) a definite veto on the Arab option for a military offensive by freezing the supply of Soviet arms. The Soviet policy of the maintenance of the status quo of "no war, no peace" was justified on the ideological ground that the Arab struggle against Israel was an integral part of the worldwide struggle against imperialism. Its success required close cooperation with the Soviet Union and final victory of socialism.[4] This ambivalence was largely responsible for the defection of Egypt from the Soviet camp in 1976.

Although the advent of strategic parity and ensuring detente between superpowers lowered the priority of the West Asian region in Soviet strategy, its immediate impact did not go beyond a tacit Soviet undertaking to prevent the outbreak of of hostilities in the region. Detente was merely a working relationship between two adversaries, not friends. It did not mean the congruence of Soviet and American interests in the region. Both the Soviet Union and United States acted from their own self-interest. None of them wanted an outcome which resulted in the diminution of its inflence. However, despite the conflict of interests and wills, the two superpowers were eventually able to act jointly in restoring peace and preserving their detente.

Buttressing the proposition about the ambivalent and compromising nature of the Soviet policy towards the Arab-Israeli conflict are certain broad conclusions regarding the Soviet crisis-behaviour and interventions in this area.[5] In the global and regional competition for influence with the United

States, the Soviet Union has often used threats of intervention to produce desired political outcomes. Soviet interventions in the West Asian crises have mostly been defensive in nature aiming at preservation, rather than destruction of the status quo.

There is by now enough literature on the Soviet interventionist behaviour. Except the Hungarian, Czechoslovakian and Afghanistan crises which occurred in 1956, 1968 and 1979 respectively and where the Soviet Union used physical force to preserve its spheres of influence, Soviet crisis behaviour has generally been cautious, moderate, low risk-taking, conservative, deliberate and rational. A study of Soviet interventionist behaviour during the Suez crisis 1956, June 1967 war, Suez crisis 1970, and the October 1973 War (Cf. Chapter III—VI of this work) reveals that the threats of Soviet intervention were moderate and defensive in character. They were couched in general and imprecise terms (barring the one issued on 31 January 1970) because of the characteristic reluctance of the Soviet leaders to commit their armed forces to areas outside the Soviet orbit. However, because of the credibility of the USSR as a superpower and uncertainty created by these threats, they were always taken seriously by the other great power and thus achieved their political objectives.

In the Suez crisis of 1956 Moscow warned against "acts of aggression" in violation of the security interests of the Soviet Union. A series of letters on 5 November 1956 from Soviet Premier N.A. Bulganin and Foreign Minister Dimitri Shepilov to the Governments of Britain, France, Israel, United States and the UN Security Council vague threats of retaliation by rockets were held out against the aggressors if they did not obey the UN General Assembly ceasefire resolution. Before the outbreak of the hostilities in the Canal Zone, Khrushchev had promised on 6 November to send "volunteers" to help Egypt. He did not repeat this threat until 10 November, four days after the ceasefire had taken place, when the threat was unlikely to arouse adverse Western response. Its effect was immediate : the USA compelled its allies to evacuate their forces from the Canal Zone to prevent the entry of the Soviets in this area.

Soviet policy during the June 1967 War was extremely cautious, non-committal and non-interventionist. After assuring themselves that the USA will not intervene in the war they silently saw the liquidation of the Egyptian army in the Sinai and did nothing to prevent it. But on 10 June, the last day of war, Premier Kosygin in a message to American President L.B. Johnson threatened to take "necessary actions, including military" if Israel did not halt its operations within a few hours. Moscow was forced to threaten verbally to prevent the advance of the Israeli army towards Damascus. Thus, the threat of intervention was strictly defensive directed to preservation of Soviet prestige.

In the Suez crisis of 1972 it was the total vulnerability of Egypt and the imminent collapse of the Nasser regime that forced the Soviets to call the attention of the Western powers to the plight of Egypt warning that if they did not stop Israel the Soviet Union will supply more arms to the victims to bolster their defences. Soviet deployment of its forces in Egypt during 1970-1972 did not have any other aim except deterrence of Israel.

The Soviet threat on 24 October 1973 to "consider the question of appropriate steps unilaterally," if a joint Soviet-American force to supervise the ceasefire of 22 October was not despatched was similarly tied closely with the preservation of the Soviet prestige. The Israeli forces had not only encircled the Egyptian Third Army located on the east bank of the Suez Canal by penetrating the west bank but also were poised for a march into Cairo. Here again the Soviet Union retreated as soon as its objective of relieving pressure on the Egyptian Third Army was achieved.

Thus, Soviet conduct in the Arab-Israel arena has reflected throughout the primacy of the Soviet national interest and an orientation towards the preservation of the status quo so long as it does not jeopardise the Soviet material interest.

REFERENCES

1. William Welch, "Soviet Expansiveness and the Its Assessment" *Journal of Conflict Resolution* 15 (3), September 1972, p. 325.
2. Cited by Andre Fontaine, *History of the Cold War* (London 1970), p. 171.

3. *Pravda Izvestia*, 4 January 1964.
4. E.g., E. Primakov's remarks on the nature of the Arab-Israeli Conflict, *SWB* I, 10 June, 1971.
5. The behaviour of one international actor towards another is described as interventionary "whenever the form of the behaviour constitutes a sharp break with then existing forms and whenever it is directed at changing or preserving the structure of political authority in the target society." J.N. Rosenau. "Intervention as a Scientific Concept" in Rosenau, ed., *The Scientific* Study of Foreign Policy (New York, 1971), p. 292.
6. Cf. M.P. Gehlen, *The Politics of Coexistence* (Bloomington, 1967) : J.F. Triska and D.D. Finley, *Soviet Foreign Policy* (New York, 1968), pp. 311 ff ; W. Philips Davison, *The Berlin Blockade* : *A Study in Cold War Politics* (Salem, NH, 1958-1980) ; and Hannes Adomeit, *Soviet Risk-Taking and Crisis Behaviour* : *A Theoretical and Empirical Analysis* (London, 1982).

Select Bibliography

Books and Articles

Adomeit, H., "Soviet Policy in the Middle East". *Soviet Studies* 27 (2), April 1972.

Andashev, V. ; and P. Oglobin, *Soviet-Arab Friendship* : What It means in Practice. Moscow : Progress Publishers, 1972.

Aspaturian, Vernon V., ed., *Process and Power in Soviet Foreign Policy*, Boston : Little, Brown, 1971.

———, "The Soviet Military-Industrial Complex : Does It Exist ?" *Journal of International Affairs* 26 (1), 1972.

Ballis, W.B., "Soviet Foreign Policy towards Developing States : The Case of Egypt". *Studies on the Soviet Union* 7 (3), 1967-68.

Bell, Coral, "The October Middle East War : A Case Study in Crisis Management during Detente". *International Affairs* (London) 50 (4), October 1974.

Belyaev, I., "Ways of Ending the Middle East Crisis". *International Affairs* (Moscow), No. 10, October 1968.

Binder, Leonard, "The Middle East as a Subordinate International System". *World Politics* 10 (3), April 1958.

Black, Cyril E., *Understanding Soviet Politics*. The Perspective of Russian History. London : West-view Press, 1986.

Bolton, A.R.C., *Soviet Middle Eastern Studies* : An Analysis and Bibliography. Oxford : Oxford University Press for Royal Institute of International Affairs, 1959.

Campbell, John C., *Defence of the Middle East*. Problems of American Policy. New York : Harper and Row, 1960.

———, "The Soviet Union and the United States in the Middle East". *Annals of the American Academy of Political and Social Science*, 401, May 1972.

Carlisle, D.S., "The Changing Soviet Perception of the Development Process in the Afro-Asian World". *Midwest Journal of Political Science* 8 (4), November 1964.

Childers, Erskine, *The Road to Suez*. A Study of Western-Arab Relations. London : MacGibbon and Kee, 1962.

Connel, John, *The Most Important Country* : The True Story of the Suez Crisis and the Events Leading to It. London ; Cassel, 1957.

Cottrell, A., "The Soviet Union as a Major Power in the Middle East : A Review of Recent Literature". *World Affairs* 123 (4), March 1971.

Cremeans, Charles D., *The Arabs and the World* : Nasser's Arab Nationalist Policy. New York : Praeger, 1963.

Current Digest of the Soviet Press, *Soviet Foreign Policy Today*. Columbus, Ohio : Current Digest of the Soviet Press, 1983.

Dallin, David J., *Soviet Foreign Policy After Stalin*. Philadelphia : J.B. Lippincott Co., 1961.

Dawisha, Adeed ; and Karen Dawisha, eds., *The Soviet Union in the Middle East* : Policies and Perspectives. London : Heinemann for Royal Institute of International Affairs 1982.

Dawisha, Karen, *Soviet Foreign Policy toward Egypt*. New York : St. Martin, 1979.

———, "Soviet Decision-making in the Middle East : The 1973 October War and the 1980 Gulf War". *International Affairs* 57 (1), Winter 1980.

———, "Soviet Policy in the Arab World : Permanent Interests and Changing Influence". *Arab Studies Quarterly* 2(1), Winter 1980.

———, "The U.S.S.R. in the Middle East : Superpower in Eclipse ? *Foreign Affairs* 61 (2), Winter 1982/83.

Dimant-Kass, I., "The Soviet Military and Soviet Policy in the Middle East, 1970-1973". *Soviet Studies* 26 (4), October 1974.

Draper, Theodore, *Israel and World Politics*. Roots of the Third Arab-Israeli War. New York : Viking Press, 1968.

Eban, Abba, *Voice of Israel*. New York : Horizon Press, 1969.

Eden, Sir Anthony, *The Memoirs* : Full Circle. London ; Cassel, 1960.

Eisenhower, Dwight D., *White House Years*. Waging Peace 1956-58. London : Heinemann, 1966.

Eytan, Walter, *The First Ten Years* : A Diplomatic History of Israel. New York : Simon and Schuster, 1958.

Finer, Herman, *Dulles over Suez*. London : Heinemann, 1964.

Fontaine, Andre, *History of the Cold War from the Korean War to the Present*. London : Secker and Warburg, 1970.

Forsythe, D.P., "The Soviets and the Arab-Israeli Conflict". *World Affairs* 134, Fall 1971.

Freedman, Robert O., *Soviet Policy toward the Middle East since 1970*. 2nd rev. ed. New York : Praeger, 1978.

———, "Soviet Policy toward the Middle East since the Invasion of Afghanistan". *Journal of International Affairs* 34 (2), Fall/Winter 1980-81.

Gehlen, M.P., *The Politics of Coexistence* : Soviet Methods and Motives. Bloomington : Indiana University Press, 1967.

Glassenapp, I.O., "Recent Developments in Soviet Policy towards Israel". *Bulletin of the Institute for the Study of* USSR 16 (4), 1969.

Glassman, Jon D., *Arms for the Arabs*. The Soviet Union and War in the Middle East. Baltimore/London : The Johns Hopkins University Press, 1975.

Golan, Galia, *Yom Kippur and After*. Cambridge : Cambridge University Press, 1977.

———, "The Soviet Union and the Israeli Action in Lebanon". *International Affairs* 59 (1), Winter 1982/83.

Goldman, Marshall I., *Soviet Foreign Aid*. New York : Praeger, 1967.

Gorbatov, O.M. ; and Cerkasskij L. Ja, *Bor'ba USR Za obespecenie procnogo i spravedlivogo mira na Bliznem Vostoke* (1867-1980). Moscow : Nauka, 1980.

Graber, Doris A., "Perceptions of the Middle East Conflict in the U.N., 1953-1965". *Journal of Conflict Resolution* 13 (4), December 1969.

Gruliow, Leo, ed., *Current Soviet Policies.* Vol. II : The Documentary Record of the 20th Communist Party Congress and Its Aftermath. New York : Praeger, 1957.

———, *Current Soviet Policies.* Vol. III : The Documentary Record of the Extraordinary 21st Communist Party Congress and Its Aftermath. New York : Columbia University Press, 1966.

Haines, C. Grove, ed., *The Threat of Soviet Imperialism.* Baltimore : Johns Hopkins University Press, 1954.

Halliday, Fred, "Chernenko's Inheritance : The Parameters of Soviet Foreign Policy." *Millennium* 13 (1), Spring 1984.

——— "The U.S.S.R. and the Persian Gulf". *Mainstream* (New Delhi) 22 (42), 16 June 1984.

Hayter, Sir William. *The Kremlin and the Embassy.* London : Hodder, 1966.

Heikal, Mohamed, *Nasser* : The Cairo Documents. London : New English Library, 1972.

———, *The Road to Ramadan.* London : Collins, 1975.

———, *Sphinx and Commissar* : The Soviet Union and the Middle East. London : Collins, 1978.

Hirschmann, Ira, *Red Star over Bethlehem* : The Soviet Influence in the Middle East. London : Arthur Barker, 1971.

Hoffmann, E.P. ; and F.J. Fleron, Jr., eds., *The Conduct of Soviet Foreign Policy.* Hawthorn, N.Y. : Aldine, 1980.

Hosmer, Steven ; and Thomas W. Wolfe. *Soviet Policy and Practice toward Third World Conflicts.* Lexington, Mass. : Lexington Books, 1983.

Hough, Jerry F., *The Struggle for the Third World.* Soviet Debates and American Options (Washington, D.C. : Brookings, 1986).

Hurewitz, J.C., ed., *Soviet-American Rivalry in the Middle East* New York : Praeger

Israeli, Raphael, ed., *The Public Diary of President Sadat.* 3 volumes. Leid. E.J. Brill, 1978-79.

Israelyan, V., ed., *Soviet Foreign Policy* : A Brief Review, 1955-65. Moscow ; Progress Publishers, 1962.

Jaber, F., "Soviet Attitudes toward Arab Revolutions : Yemen, Algeria, Iraq, Palestine". *Middle East Forum* 46 (4), 1972.

Johnson, Lyndon B., *The Vantage Point*. Perspective of the Presidency 1963-1969. Delhi: Vikas (1971) 1972.

Joshua, Wynfred: and Stephen P. Gilbert, *Arms for the Third World*: Soviet Military Aid Diplomacy. Baltimore: The Johns Hopkins University Press, 1969.

Juviller, Peter H.; and Henry W. Morton, eds., *Soviet Policy-Making*: Studies of Communism in Transition. New York Praeger, 1967.

Kahn, R.A., Israel and the Soviet Union: a review of postwar relations". *Grbis* 9 (4). Winter 1966.

Khalidi, Rashid, *The Soviet Union and the Middle East 1980s*. Beirut: Institute for Palestine Studies, 1980.

Khrushchev, Nikita S., *Speechcs and Interviews on World Problems*. Moscow: Foreign Languages Publishing House, 1958.

Kissinger, Henry A., *Years of Upheaval*. New Delhi: Vikas, 1981.

Kremnyev, Mikhail, "The Non-Aligned Countries and World Politics". *World Marxist Review* 6 (4), April 1963.

Lall, Arthur S., *The U.N. and the Middle East Crisis, 1967*. New York/London: Columbia University Press, 1970.

Laqueur, Walter Z., *Communism and Nationalism in the Middle East*. London: Routledge & Kegan Paul, 1956.

———, *The Soviet Union and the Middle East*. London: Routledge & Kegan Paul, 1959.

———, *Road to War 1967*; the origins of the Arab-Israeli Conflict, London: Weidenfeld and Nicolson, 1968.

———, *The Struggle for the Middle East*: The Soviet Union in the Mediterranean 1958-1968. New York: MacMillan, 1969.

———, *Confrontation*: The Middle East and World Politics. London: Abacus, 1974.

Lederer, Ivo J.; and Wayne S. Vucinich, *The Soviet Union and the Middle East*: The Post-World War II Era. Stanford: Hoover Institution Press, 1974.

Leitenberg, Milton; and Gabriel Sheffer eds., *Great Power Intervention in the Middle East*. New York: Pergamon Press, 1979.

Lenczowski, George, *Soviet Advances in the Middle East*. Washington, D.C.: American Enterprise Institute for Public Policy Research, 1972.

London, Kurt, ed., *The Soviet Union*: A Half Century of Communism. Baltimore: The Johns Hopkins University Press, 1968.

McLaurin, R.D., *The Middle East in Soviet Policy*. Lexington, Books, 1975.

Meir, Golda, *My Life*. London: Weidenfeld and Nicolson, 1975.

Moncrief, Anthony; and Peter Calvocoressi, eds., *Suez Ten Years After*. Broadcasts from the B.B.C. Third Programme. London: B.B.C., 1967.

Nasser, Gamal A., Interview on 1956 Crisis. *Sunday Times*, 17 June, 24 June and 1 July 1962.

Nixon, Richard M., *Memoirs*. New York: Crosset & Dunlop, 1978.

Nolt, A.H., "Arab Nationalism and the Cold War" *Yale Review* 49 (1), Autumn 1959.

Papp, Daniel S., *Soviet Perceptions of the Developing World in the 1980s*: The Ideological Basis (Lexington, Mass Lexington Book 1985).

———, *Decade of Decisions*: American Policy towards the Arab-Israeli Conflict, 1967-1976. Berkeley/London: University of California Press, 1977.

Porter, Bruce D., *The U.S.S.R. in Third World Conflicts*. Soviet Arms and Diplomacy in Local Wars, 1954-1984. New York: Cambridge University Press, 1983.

Pranger, Robert J., *Six U.S. Perspectives on Soviet Foreign Policy Intentions*. Washington, D.C.: American Enterprise Institute for Public Policy Research, 1979.

Primakov, Y., "The Fourth Arab-Israeli War". *World Marxist Review* 16 (12), December 1973.

Quandt, William B., "Soviet Policy in the October Middle East War I". *International Affairs* 53 (3), July 1977.

———, "Soviet Policy in the October Middle East War II" *International Affairs* 53 (4), October 1977.

Ra'anan, Uri, *The USSR Arms and the Third World*: Case Studies in Soviet Foreign Policy. Cambridge, Mass./ London: MIT Press, 1970.

———, "The USSR and the Middle East: Some Reflections on the Soviet Decision-Making Process". *Orbis* 17 (3), 1973.

Riad, Mahmoud, *The Struggle for Peace in the Middle East*. London: Quartet Books, 1981.

Robertson, Terrence, *Crisis*: The Inside Story of the Suez Conspiracy. London: Hutchinson, 1965.

Rubenstein, Alvin Z., *Red Star on the Nile*: Soviet-Egyptian Influence Relationship since the June War. Princeton, N.J.: Princeton University Press, 1977.

Rush, Myron, *International Situation and Soviet Foreign Policy*. Columbus, Ohio: Charles E. Merrill, 1970.

Sadat, Anwar el—, *In Search of Identity*: An Autobiography. London: Collins, 1978.

Saikowski, Charlotte; and Leo Gruliow, eds., *Current Soviet Policies*. Vol. IV: The Documentary Record of the 22nd Congress of the Communist Party of the Soviet Union. New York: Columbia University Press, 1962.

Seale, Patrick, *The Struggle for Syria*: a study of post-war Arab politics, 1945-58. London: Oxford University Press, 1965.

Sella, Amnon *Soviet Political and Military Conduct in the Middle East*. London: MacMillan, 1981.

Shulman, M.D., *Soviet Foreign Policy Reappraised*. Cambridge, Mass.: Harvard University Press, 1963.

———, "Recent Soviet Foreign Policy: Some Patterns in Retrospect". *Journal of International Affairs* 22 (1), 1968.

Smolansky, Oles M., "Moscow and the Persian Gulf: An Analysis of Soviet Ambitions and Potential". *Orbis* 14 (1), Spring 1970.

———, *The Soviet Union and Arab East under Khrushchev*. Bucknell: Bucknell University Press, 1974.

Sontag, John P., "Internationalism and Soviet Foreign Policy". *Review of Politics* 32 (1), January 1970.

Spechler, Dina Rome, "The USSR and Third-World Conflicts : Domestic Debate and Soviet Policy in the Middle East, 1967-1973 *World Politics* 38 (3), April 1986.

Stephens, Robert, *Nasser.* A Political Biography. London : Allen Lane/The Penguin Press, 1971.

Teller, Jud L., *The Kremlin, the Jews and the Middle East.* New York: Thomas Yoseloff, 1957.

Thomas, Hugh, *The Suez Affair.* London: Weidenfeld and Nicolson, 1967. A revised edition was published as a Pelican book in 1970.

Thornton, Thomas P., *The Third World in Soviet Perspective.* 2nd ed. Princeton. N.J. : Princeton University Press, 1984.

Triska, Jan F., "A Model for Study of Soviet Foreign Policy". *American Political Science Review* 52 (1), March 1958.

———; and David D. Finely, *Soviet Foreign Policy.* New York : Mac-Millan, 1968.

Ulam, Adam B., "Soviet Ideology and Soviet Foreign Policy. W. *World Politics* 11 (2), January 1959.

———, *Expansion and Coexistence.* Soviet Foreign Policy, 1917 to 1973. 2nd ed. New York : Harper and Row, 1974.

Valkenier, E.K. "Trends in Soviet Research on the Developing Countries in W. Raymond Duncan, ed., *Soviet Policy in Developing Countries*, Waltham, Mass. : Ginn-Blaisdell, 1981.

Ulianovsky, Rostislav, *Present-Day Problems in Asia and Africa.* Moscow : Progress Publishers, 1980.

U.S.S.R., *The Policy of the Soviet Union in the Arab World.* A short collection of foreign policy documents. Moscow : Progress Publishers, 1975.

U.S.S.R., *24th Congress of the Communist Party of the Soviet Union.* Moscow : Novosti Press Agency Publishing House, 1971.

United Nations, Security Council, *Official Records.*

———, General Assembly, *Official Records.*

United Nations Yearbooks.

Welch, William, "The Sources of Soviet Conduct : A Note on Method". *Background* 6 (4), Winter 1963.

———, *American Images of Soviet Foreign Policy*. An Inquiry into Recent Appraisals from the Academic Community. New Haven/London : Yale University Press, 1970.

———; and Jan F. Triska, "Soviet Foreign Policy Studies and Foreign Policy Models". *World Politics* 23 (4), July 1971.

Whetten, Lawrence L., *The Canal War* : Four-Power Conflict in the Middle East. London : MIT Press, 1974.

———, *The Arab-Israeli Dispute* : Great Power Behaviour. London : International Institute for Strategic Studies, 1976-77.

———, "Soviet-Syrian Moves in the Middle East". *Round Table* 279, July 1980.

Wint, Guy ; and Peter Calvocoressi, *Middle East Crisis* Harmondsworth : Penguin Books, 1957.

Yost, Charles W., "The Arab-Israeli War. How It Began". *Foreign Affairs* 46 (2), January 1968.

Zamostny, Thomas J., "Moscow and the Third World : Recent Trends in Soviet Thinking". *Soviet Studies* 36 (2), April 1984.

Zimmerman, William, *Soviet Perspectives on International Relations* 1956-1967. Princeton, N.J. : Princeton University Press, 1969.

———, "What Do Scholars Know about Soviet Foreign Policy ?". *International Journal* 37, Spring 1982.

Periodicals

Cairo Press Review. d. Cairo.

Current Digest of the Soviet Press. w. Columbus, Ohio.

Current History. m. Philadelphia.

Daily Review. d. (Translations from the Soviet Press). New Delhi : Novosti Press Agency.

Department of State Bulletin. w. Washington, D.C.

Economist. w. London.

Egyptian Gazette. d. Cairo.

International Affairs. m. Moscow.

Keesings Contemporary Archives. w. London.

Middle East International. m. London.

Mizan. bi/m. London.
New Left Review. bi/m. London.
New Middle East. m. London.
New Times. w. Moscow.
New York Times. d. New York.
Newsweek. w. Livingstone, N.J.
Review of International Affairs. w. Belgrade.
Soviet News. 3/w. London.
Summary of World Broadcast Part I, Soviet Union and Eastern Europe ; Part IV, Middle East and Africa. d. Reading, England : BBC.
Survival. Bi/m. London.
The Time. w. Chicago.
The Times. d. London.
U.N. Monthly Chronicle. m. New York.
U.S. News and World Report. w. Boulder, Co.
World Marxist Review m. Toronto.
World Press Review. m. Farmingdale, N.J.
World Today. m. London.

INDEX

The Arab-Israeli Confiict

The Armistice Agreements (1949) 23, 24, 63
The Armistice Borders, 128
The Anglo-Egyptian Treaty (1954), 33
The Soviet-Egyptian Arms Deal (1955), 26, 39
The French-Israeli Arms Deal, 39
The Baghdad Pact (1955), 38
Dayan on Israeli Borders, 128
Eisenhower on the Suez War, 39,47
Eytan on Israeli Borders, 22-23, 63-64, 130-131
The Glassboro Summit (1967), 79
Jarring as Mediator in, 86, 97, 104 129
Ra'anan on Arms Deal (1955), 39, 40, 65
The Tripartite Declaration (1950), 23, 28
The UNRWA, 129, 130
The Straits of Tiran, 73-74
Withdrawal of the UNEF, 73
Johnson on Israeli Motives during 1967, 72, 75-76, 79, 152
The War of 1948, 22-23
The Suez War (1956), 36-65
The War of 1967, 31, 75-78
The Suez Crisis (1970), 92-97
The War of 1973, 123-124
The Lebanese Crisis (1982), 142
Arafat, Yasser, 146
Brezhnev, Leonid 99, 122, 138
Dobrynin, Anatoli, 115-117
Dulles, John Foster, 38, 50
Eban, Abba, 65, 72
Eden, Sir Anthony, 42, 43, 45, 47, 51, 55, 60
Fedorenko, Nikolai, 74, 76
Gorbachev, Mikhail, 143-146
Gorshkov, Sergei, 29
Gromyko, Andrei, 78, 88, 135, 142
Johnson, Lyndon B., 72, 76, 79
Khrushchev, Nikita S., 6, 29, 64
Kissinger, Henry A., 113, 115, 118, 120, 123
Kosygin, Aexei, 30, 64, 78, 79, 152
Meire, Golda, 22, 88, 96, 101
Nasser, Gamal A., 31, 50, 92, 97-98
Nixon, Richard M., 91, 96, 97, 112, 118, 132

Peace Plans for West Asia

UN General Assembly Resolution 194 (III), 22, 141

UN Security Council Resolution 242, 17-18, 90, 96, 128, 132, 137, 141
Rogers' Peace Plan, 90-91, 96-100
Meir on Rogers' Initiative, 88, 96
Parimakov on Soviet Proposals, 112, 136, 140, 151
UN Security Council Resolution 338, 90, 118, 145
Brezhnev on Soviet Intentions during 1973, 99, 112, 138
Soviet-American Statement of 1977, 139, 142, 145
Egyptian-Israeli Peace Treaty (1979) 33, 139
Soviet Statement of 1984, 226
Riad, Mahmoud, 101
Sadat, Muhammad Anwar El-, 100, 105, 106, 109, 114, 115, 116, 125, 139 Journey to Jerusalem (1977), 139
Sadeg, Muhamed, 112
San Clement Summit (1973), 112
Shepilov, Dimitriyi, 40
Sidqi, Aziz, 107, 112

Soviet Foreign Policy, Nature of

Edmonds on, 2
Bell on 2, 6
Zimmerman on 2
Ideology and Interest in, 3-8
Aspaturian on, 7, 17, 18, 113, 123 145-146
Welch on, 145
Rubenstein on, 72, 96, 98-99, 117, 122
Lall on Soviet Motives during 1967, 72, 79
Laqueur on Soviet Motives during 1967, 72-79
Heikal on Soviet Role during 1967, 72, 94, 98, 101, 115, 117
Whetten on Soviet Actions during 1967, 71, 77, 79, 95, 99, 106, 110, 115
Deutscher in Stalin's Support to Israel, 21
Twentieth Congress of the Communist Party of the Soviet Union, 21
Belyaev on, 136, 141
Kurt London on, 4
Galia Golan on, 116, 122
Hayter on, 60

The Soviet Union and the Arab-Israeli Conflict

The Bolshevik Attitude towards Zionism, 19
Myrskiy on the Palestine Problem, 138
The Partition of Palestine, 21
The War of 1948, 22-23
Soviet Recognition of Israel, 22
Soviet Guarantee of Israeli Statehood, 127
Reversal of Soviet Policy towards Israel, 23-24, 26
Reaction to the Tripartite Declaration (1950), 24, 39
Reaction to the Baghdad Pact (1955), 26
The Building of the Aswan Dam 40-41, 58
The Suez War (1956), 41, 56-65, 152
The Syrian Crisis (1966), 69-75
On Withdrawal of the UNEF, 73
The War of 1967, 31, 75-78
The UN Security Council Resolution 242, 79
Role in the Jordanian Crisis (1970), 92-95
Participation in the Four-Power Talks, 90
Role in the War of Attrition, 96-97
Role in the Suez Crisis (1970), 97, 122
Proposal for Partial Settlement, 100

Soviet-Egyptian Treaty of Friendship and Cooperation (1971), 104-108, 113-114, 123
Role during the War of 1973, 123, 124
Soviet Interventionist Behaviour, 150-151
On the UN Security Council Resolution 338, 90, 118, 145
On Israeli Violation of Ceasefire on 22 October 1973, 120, 152
On Direct Negotiations between Arabs and Israel, 127
The Issue of Boundaries, 128
The Problem of Palestinian Refugees, 128
The Status of Jerusalem, 23, 130-131
The Jordan River Waters, 131
The International Waterways, 131
Soviet Struggle for a Political Settlement, 132-137
Attitude towards the Palestinian Movement, 140
Inaction during the Lebanese Crisis of 1982, 142
Renewed Call for an International Conference, 142
The Gorbachev Era in Soviet Foreign Policy, 146

Stalin, Joseph, 19, 21, 25

Vinogradov, V.A., 115
Vyshinsky, Andrei A., 129

West Asia

Geostrategic Significance of, 12-14
Ideological Movements in, 14-15
Soviet Policy during 1945-55, 16 33, during 1956-66, 63-65, during 1968-72, 83-103, during 1973-88, 113-123, 137-146
American Policy in, 15, 85, 100-101
The Cold War in, 23, 24, 37
Soviet-American Detente in, 107 122, 151
Comintern Approach to, 17-18
The Soviet Union as a Regional Power in, 17, 79, 112, 142
The Soviet Union as a Mediterranean Power, 28-30
Soviet Base Facilities in Egypt, 29
Soviet-Egyptian Treaty of 1971, 108
Expulsion of Soviet Advisers from Egypt, 109
Western Embargo on Arms to, 95
Emigration of Russian Jews to Israel, 132